FOOD *for the* HEART

FOOD *for the* HEART

111 message bites

KAMRAN YARAEI

Food for the Heart
by Kamran Yaraei

Printed in the United States of America

ISBN 978-1-60791-449-5

Cover design: Joel Davis, Cross and Crown Productions, www.cacpro.com
Interior design: projectluz.com
www.xulonpress.com

Contents

Catalogue of Courses

Foreword
by Suzy Yaraei

When I first introduced Kamaran to a friend of mine who is a well respected man of God, he placed his hand on Kamran's heart and said, "You have been given a poetic heart." This simple word could not have been more true. He talks, writes, eats, and drinks the poetic, sweeping romance of God the Father, Son, and Holy Spirit that few ever discover. Friends and family will all attest to this. It is a wonder to listen to him tell of his relationship and conversations with God as if Jesus will walk into the room any minute and sweep us off our feet.

One day I was having an ugly day, as we gals all do occasionally, and he asked me what was wrong. I said I felt really ugly. He asked me how I came to this conclusion. I said rather wryly, "I looked in the mirror." He looked at me with burning love and said, "I am your mirror." It was like Jesus was talking straight to my heart and spirit. I melted.

Since his transformation in 2000, Kamran has spent much of his time walking and conversing with God, and he records these experiences faithfully in journals.

His first book is a compilation of some of the simple yet powerful messages he has received. These messages will help us all to connect to God in a fresh way. They will bring us back to our first love. They will help new believers know a living God who loves us beyond description. These timeless lessons are practical, yet they carry us into the heavenly heart of a mysterious and passionate God. We need this nourishment for our minds, souls, spirits, and bodies as well as our hearts.

Some of us are able to feed our stomachs at every whim. Some of us are not that blessed. All of us need food for our hearts from the heart of God. Taste and see how good the Lord really is through one man's journey to fill these pages with all delights from His Father's table.

Fill yourself up and let the Father, Son, and Holy Spirit sweep you off your feet!

Prologue

I want to talk to you about my experience with God Almighty
and the journey that I walked as a Shiite Muslim.
When I came to this earth, I landed in a small city in northern Iran.
It was not my decision to be there.
God wanted me to be there and I was there on time.

Where did you land, my friend?
Did you choose to be there, or was it your destiny?

The country that I landed in has a Muslim religion.
When I grew old enough to pay attention to my heart's desire to know the
Creator,
I was told that Allah is God and Islam is the true religion.
Was it my fault that I was exposed to Islam?
I leave the answer to you.

All I wanted was to know God and I was told His name was Allah.
I was also told many other things about the god of Islam,
and I believed what I was told.
What do you think of me now?

For thirty-three years, I thought Almighty God was
what Islam described Him to be.
I didn't want to kill anyone.
I was just an average Muslim who wanted to be a good person,
have a relationship with God, and make it to heaven.

I believe that 90 percent of Muslims never think to hurt anyone,
or to kill, or to be involved in acts of terrorism.
I was one of those average Muslims.
Most of my life I pursued God and wanted to have Him in my life.
My dream was to get His attention,
to move Him to look at me and be pleased with me, my good works,
and my prayer five times a day.

I just wanted to know God and be known by Him.
Since I landed in Iran in a Shiite Muslim family, all I knew was Islam.
I had many Shiite Muslims around me.

When you started to listen to your heart's desire for God,
who was around you?
What kind of information did you receive about God?
What incidents took place to form your belief or unbelief?
What were you exposed to?

Let's talk about the minority of Muslims who end up as terrorists.
Who do you think they had around them?
Are they all bad?
Are we all good?
What should we do about our differences?
What should we do about the judgments we have against each other?
Who is right and who is wrong?
Is life about being right or wrong, or is it about love?

On January 21, 2000, Jesus appeared to me and I gave Him my heart.
I wanted to tell everyone about Him.
It looked like Christ was not in a hurry to use me to
spread the good news at first.
I begged Him many times to release me to tell Muslims about Him,
but He had a different plan for my heart in that season.
He allowed me to walk with Him day and night.
He took my heart to the school of love,
but my heart was so afraid and hurt.
I was not a very good student of love,
but my teacher was patient with me.
It makes sense that my teacher was patient because love is patient,
and love was my teacher.
After eight years of Jesus working on my heart,
I now feel personally released to share the good news of Christ with others.

I was so surprised and touched when one day I heard this in my heart:
"Close your eyes and ask your heart this question:
Am I willing to physically lay my life down

for the person I share the gospel of love with?"
The answer in my heart was no.

Then I heard this:
"Are you willing to meditate on laying your life down
for the one you give the good news of salvation to?"
"Yes, I am willing to meditate on it," I said.

Later I learned that the meditation of laying down my physical life
for those I share the good news with will open my heart
to receive supernatural love from above for them.

"Greater love has no one than this, that one lay down his life for his friends"

(JOHN 15:13).

"I don't necessarily call myself a friend of Muslims," one may say.
"To be honest, I don't feel like being their friend," another may say.
But wait a minute.
Jesus was sweating blood in the garden
before being nailed on the cross for all of mankind,
which includes Muslims too.
He didn't feel like going to the cross,
but He endured and went beyond His feelings
and pain because He is love.
His love gave Him the ability to finish the job that had to be done.
He taught us how to do the same.
Love can believe all things, endure all things, and get the job done.

[Love] bears all things, believes all things, hopes all things, endures all things.
Love never fails; but if there are gifts of prophecy, they will be done away;
if there are tongues, they will cease; if there is knowledge, it will be done away

(I CORINTHIANS 13:7-8).

Some may say, "Come on, this is the twenty-first century.
Wake up and see reality.
Poetry and nice writing will not get the job done.
We need to show those Muslims that they are wrong.

We need to stop them as soon as possible or they will take over."

I am writing this because one of you reached out to me
and shared the gospel with me.
I was a Shiite Muslim.

I am the product of God's love through you, my friend.
You changed my life and gave me hope, my friend.
You hugged me when I so desperately needed it.
You poured into me when I was thirsty and dry,
and I bless you in His name.

May you and your country prosper and be blessed.
May your children's children see God's face and be blessed,
my fellow Americans.
Thank you for sharing the love of God with me.
Now I want to share with you some of the nourishment
I have received from our precious Jesus.

1

Unconditional Evangelism

The most effective form of giving is unconditional giving,
but many of us give the good news of salvation conditionally.
Many of us share the message of salvation with others,
expecting them to give their hearts to Jesus upon
hearing the good news.
If they do not, we become unhappy, unsatisfied,
and unnecessarily burdened
because we expected to get something back from them.
We focus more on the person's submission than on the good news.

God never asked us to force people into His kingdom.
He only asked us to share His kingdom with others
and to extend them an invitation.
If you have ever evangelized on a conditional basis,
I would like to introduce to you a new method:
unconditional evangelism.

Conditional evangelism is giving the good news of salvation to another person
with the expectation of their submission.
In this kind of giving, we give to receive something back,
which opens the door for limitation and suspicion.
Unconditional evangelism is giving the good news of salvation
without any expectations.
Our focus is on giving the good news, not receiving submission.
We need to be like John the Baptist,
preparing the way for the Lord to come in
through our unconditional love and evangelism.

There is such beauty and freedom in unconditional acts of love and giving.
Unconditional giving attracts the Lord and unbelievers.
Unconditional giving is always welcome among people of any culture
or background.

God's love is not conditional.
The power of His unconditional love made the way for us to be saved.
So why do we make our evangelism conditional?
Let us share the gospel of Christ with others
and not concentrate on their responses.
Let us focus on giving the good news and leave the rest to Jesus.
We are called to share God's good news
and love with others unconditionally.

Lord Jesus, help us to share You with others unconditionally
as Your Father shared You with us.

2

Will You Love Me?

To My Fellow Muslims

You are right that blood must be shed
to pay for the transgressions of those who are against God Almighty,
those who blaspheme Him and commit horrible crimes.
Yes, because of God's righteousness, justice, and sovereignty,
sin must be atoned through bloodshed.
(Most sacrifices involve shedding the blood of lambs or other animals.
Even those who worship idols sacrifice with bloodshed.)

Have you ever heard the story of the kings who disguised themselves
by putting on poor people's clothing
and went among their people in order to help them?
Is it possible that God Almighty, the Maker of all, got so angry over our sins
that He chose to put on the flesh of a human being
so He could shed His own blood to finish it all?

Is it possible that God came to us to shed not our blood but His own?
Can we give Him that much credit?
Could God Almighty have humbled Himself
to the point of putting on our flesh as His clothing?

Is it possible for God to love everyone—even sinners—and hate only the sin itself?
Why is it so hard to believe that God is capable of loving us unconditionally?
Why is it so hard to believe that He would shed His own blood
in order to save us from judgment?

Is it possible that God was misrepresented to some of us?
Is it possible that He wants to show Himself to us as He is?

My fellow Muslim, I love you.
Will you love me?
I love you even if you don't believe Jesus shed His blood.
Will you love me even if I don't believe what you believe?

3

Fear and Judgment Bring Separation

Fear will always bring separation.
Our enemy Satan will use fear of man to separate us from one another.
We naturally try to distance ourselves from those we are afraid of.
This can happen in marriages, friendships, families, churches, etc.
How can we love one another if we are afraid of each other?
For the sake of love, don't be afraid of others.
Overcome your fear so that you may love.
When we push fear out of our hearts, we open ourselves up for more love.

Judgment will also cause separation.
If you look at Islam and Christianity,
you can see that Satan brought judgment and fear
between Christians and Muslims in order to separate them.
Muslims have judgments against Christianity,
and Christians have fear of Muslims in their hearts.
How can we love the unsaved and Muslims if we are afraid of them?
Why are we separating ourselves from Muslims?
Why is the enemy planting so much fear in our hearts toward them?
He wants to separate us.

Be wise.
When you see fear, know that separation is
just around the corner of your heart.
When we push the fear of Muslims out of our hearts,
we open ourselves to the love of God for them.
And when we start to truly love them,
the love of God in us will cancel their judgment against us.

Let us stop calling them Muslims and call them our Muslim brothers.
Aren't we all children of Adam and Eve?
Aren't we all children of Abraham?
They are our brothers.

4

The Triangle of Hearts

After I gave my heart to Jesus,
He allowed me to see and travel into His heart.
Then He allowed me to travel into my own heart.
Now I feel that He wants me to pay attention to other people's hearts.

Before Christ came into my heart,
I never knew God's heart or my own heart.
After He came into my heart, I began to pay attention.
Now is the time to see people's hearts
no matter which background or belief system they are from.

May we all pay attention to the triangle of hearts.
The first step is to see God's heart.
The second is to see your own heart.
The third step is to see other people's hearts.

Understanding God's heart, our own hearts,
and other people's hearts is crucial to our peace.

How much do we understand God's heart?
How much do we understand our own hearts?
How much do we understand each others' hearts?

How much does a Palestinian understand the heart of a Jew?
How much does a Jew understand the heart of a Palestinian?
As Christians, how much do we really understand the heart of a Muslim?
How much do we understand the hearts of people?
If we ask Christ into our hearts and allow
Him to show us *the triangle of hearts*,
we will be changed.

5

Treat Your Heart as You Treat Jesus

Our hearts should be well maintained and protected.
What are we feeding our hearts?
How are we treating our hearts?
You should *treat your heart as you treat Jesus.*

Start a friendship with your own heart.
Friendship with your heart is friendship with Jesus,
because He lives in your heart.
The way you treat your heart is the way you are treating Christ.
Are you treating your heart well?
Your heart is Jesus.
He not only lives in your heart, He *is* your heart.
Respect your heart as you respect Christ.

Respect can be defined as:
"a feeling of deep admiration for someone or something elicited
by their abilities, qualities, or achievements;
agree to recognize and abide by (a legal requirement)"
(Apple Dictionary).

What does it mean to respect our hearts?
Our hearts are God's temple.
Shouldn't we respect His temple?
In the Old Testament He came to His temple,
but now He abides in His temple.
I wish we could see the value of holding God's Spirit in our hearts.
When we ignore our hearts,
we are ignoring Jesus and keeping religion in our minds.
Let us treat our hearts with respect.
Let us not abuse our hearts with selfishness, greed, pride, fear,
unstoppable desires and wants, unforgiveness, anger, etc.

We are feeding Christ whatever we feed our hearts.
The way we treat our hearts and other people's hearts
is the way we are treating Christ.

In her book, *In the Heart of the World*, Mother Teresa prays this prayer:

"O Jesus, You who suffer,
grant that today and every day I may be able to see You
in the person of Your sick ones and that,
by offering them my care, I may serve You.
Grant that, even if You are hidden under the
unattractive disguise of anger, of crime,
or of madness, I may recognize You and say,
'Jesus, You who suffer, how sweet it is to serve You.'"

Doubt, lack of faith, anger, selfishness, hopelessness,
and greed will hurt our hearts.
Even an unsaved person knows that these things will hurt their heart.
For His sake, let us reject those things.
Please treat your heart well.

Christ became your heart.
Treat Him well, my friend.

6

The Candles in Our Hearts

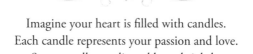

Imagine your heart is filled with candles.
Each candle represents your passion and love.
Some candles are lit and burn brightly,
while others have been blown out and have grown cold.

There was a time when all of the candles in our hearts burned brightly.

There is always a force that wants to come in and blow out your candles.
The enemy doesn't want to see light and fire in your heart
because he hates light.
It is very important to go to the Lord every day
and ask Him to light your passion and love again and again and again.

If you have an offense against someone and you haven't forgiven them,
a candle in your heart has been blown out.
Your offense gives the enemy the right to come in
and blow out your candle of passion and love toward that person.
Praying for the person will open the door
for the Lord to come in and light that candle again.

The Lord will light every candle that has been blown out,
but first you have to look at each candle
and do your part through prayer and forgiveness.

"I have come to cast fire upon the earth;
and how I wish it were already kindled!"

(LUKE 12:49)

"But I say to you, love your enemies and pray for those who persecute you"

(MATTHEW 5:44).

Ask the Lord to search your heart
and show you the candles that have been blown out.
One by one, start to bless the people represented
by each candle and pray for them.
Through your prayers you will open the door
for the Lord to come in and relight those candles.

In my personal experience, it's almost impossible to forgive someone
if I don't pray for them and bless them.
Our prayers and blessings toward people who have hurt us
will help us to easily forgive them and will fill our hearts
with fire and light again.

7

Gaining True Life

Is there a process we must go through to gain true life?
We want to see and experience true life in our relationships,
marriages, work places, and finances.
But in any relationship, or any situation,
we cannot truly see life until we learn to die.

Unless we die, we can't truly live.
Our human nature wants to escape from this reality.
Most of us think that learning how to live is so valuable;
few of us see the value of dying.

Living for ourselves is a dangerous business.
Living for self will attract all evil.
Living for self will attract fear, anxiety, weariness, greed,
selfishness, restlessness, pride, and arrogance.

Living for Christ will attract the Spirit of the Lord, true love, peace, joy,
humility, boldness, courage, selflessness, and a passionate heart.
Learn to live for Him, not for yourself.

To live for Jesus is to die to self.
Learn to die to self in order to gain true life.
We must learn this, my brothers and sisters.
Learn to die and He will not let you stay dead forever.
He will lift you up and resurrect you even in this life.
Give value to this matter of dying.
Learn this lesson with great joy.

**Then Jesus said to His disciples,
If anyone desires to be My disciple, let him deny himself
[disregard, lose sight of, and forget himself and his own interests]
and take up his cross and follow Me**

[cleave steadfastly to Me, conform wholly to My example
in living and, if need be, in dying, also].

For whoever is bent on saving his [temporal] life
[his comfort and security here] shall lose it [eternal life];
and whoever loses his life [his comfort and security here]
for My sake shall find it [life everlasting].
For what will it profit a man if he gains the whole world and forfeits his life
[his blessed life in the kingdom of God]?
Or what would a man give as an exchange for his [blessed] life
[in the kingdom of God]?

(MATTHEW 16:24-26 AMP)

8

He Comes to Kill

When facing a thief with a gun in our houses or workplaces,
we think that if we give him all of our money,
then he will leave us alone and let us live.
Sometimes we have the same mindset when we meet Jesus.
We believe that if we give everything we have to the Lord,
and serve Him well, then He might just let us live.

But the point is this:
The Lord doesn't come to steal, but to kill.
He is not after our possessions,
He is after our flesh—our old, sinful nature.
The Lord will use all of our daily struggles to kill our flesh.
Our good works and giving will not stop Him from doing this.

**"Whoever seeks to keep his life will lose it,
and whoever loses his life will preserve it"**

(LUKE 17:33).

It is very important to know that as we get closer to the Lord,
we get closer to the death of our flesh.
This should be great news to us.
He wants us to get close enough that He can kill our old nature,
which is thoroughly described in Galatians 5:19-20:

**Now the works of the flesh are evident, which are:
adultery, fornication, uncleanness, lewdness,
idolatry, sorcery, hatred, contentions, jealousies,
outbursts of wrath, selfish ambitions... (NKJV).**

The Lord not only wants to destroy sin,
He wants to kill the nature that carries these fleshly works.

As more of our old nature dies,
more of Jesus' nature will live in us and flow out of us.

"He must increase, but I must decrease"

(JOHN 3:30).

I believe that most of Jesus' commandments were designed
to make our fleshly nature uncomfortable and eventually kill it.

"You have heard that it was said, 'An eye for an eye, and a tooth for a tooth.'
"But I say to you, do not resist an evil person;
but whoever slaps you on your right cheek, turn the other to him also.
"You have heard that it was said,
'You shall love your neighbor and hate your enemy.'
"But I say to you, love your enemies..."

(MATTHEW 5:38-39, 43-44).

I used to think that if I obeyed Jesus I would become more holy.
Now I know that if I obey the Lord, my flesh will die.
I used to be afraid of anything that would bring discomfort to my flesh.
Now I welcome the idea because I see the fruits of dying to myself.

This is a process that takes time,
and if we allow Him to do it, He will make us more like Him.
Do Your work, Jesus Christ.
I am ready for You.
I love You, Jesus.

9

A New Body—in Heaven and on Earth

As God's children we will one day receive a new, glorified body in heaven—
a new body that will help us stand in God's presence and see Him as He is.
But we are entering the time when God's presence will manifest here on earth
on a higher and different level than we've known.

How will our earthly bodies be able to handle His presence
on such a high level?
Could it be that He is offering us new bodies on earth
that we can put on now to carry His presence around?

Yes!
He is offering us new bodies.
In fact, He offered us new bodies 2,000 years ago.
The new body is love.
Love can carry His presence on such a high level.
Yes, our new bodies on earth are love.

Holy Spirit, we ask You to help us put on our new bodies of love here on earth,
every single day and every single moment.
We want to carry the presence of God everywhere.
Help us to get comfortable in our new bodies.
We need Your help, and we love You very much.
We thank You so much for our new bodies.
We clothe ourselves in Your love.

And beyond all these things put on love, which is the perfect bond of unity

(COLOSSIANS 3:14).

10

God Alone Grants Repentance

God alone has the power to grant,
and when He does, no one can stop Him.
Ask Him to open your eyes to see that He is the One
who can grant you anything you need.

The Bible says that God is the One who grants repentance.

**with gentleness correcting those who are in opposition,
if perhaps God may grant them repentance leading
to the knowledge of the truth**

(II TIMOTHY 2:25).

Sometimes we get angry at people who are ignorant and don't want to repent,
but how can they repent if it was not granted to them by the Lord?

Jesus also spoke of this in the Book of John:

**And He said, this is why I told you that no one can come to Me
unless it is granted him [unless he is enabled to do so] by the Father**

(JOHN 6:65 AMP).

May the Lord grant us love, passion, forgiveness
toward each other, humility, repentance,
the fruit of His Spirit, brotherly love, health,
wealth, submission to the cross, longsuffering, wisdom,
a heart after His heart, authority, discernment, and patience.

Start asking Him to grant you godly desires,
love, and anything else you need.
Ask Him to grant you a desire to worship Him in Spirit and truth.
Ask Him to grant you freedom in those areas that you can't get free.
But especially ask Him to *grant you a heart of true repentance*.

11

Trusting God

We don't have to understand God in order to trust Him.
Instead, we must trust God in order to understand Him.
Trust birthed out of our own understanding can be shaken.

Don't waste your life trying to gain understanding in order to trust God.
Spend your life *trusting God in all situations*
so that you may understand many things.

The foundation of our understanding should be our trust
toward the Lord.
Always seek understanding and wisdom,
but remember to use your unshakable trust in the Lord as a foundation.

Help us beautiful Jesus to trust You more through Your Holy Spirit.
We love You.

12

Disappointment

When we put our hope in people or in anything other than the Lord,
we set ourselves up for great disappointments.
Disappointment will usually cause anger, frustration,
depression, and even hopelessness.
We are as guilty as those who disappoint us because
we have put our hope in them.
We are called to love others, not put our hope in them.
Just imagine if the Lord had put His hope in Adam and Eve;
it would have been a disaster.

The greater the hope that we put in people,
the greater our disappointment will be.
I have disappointed myself many times
because I put my hope in my strength, gifting, and abilities.
It is very important to let the Lord be our hope and nothing else.

We will face disappointment all of our lives
until we learn to put our hope in the Lord.
Let us collect our hope from different places and give it all to Him.
When we stop putting our hope in people or things,
then the Lord will use them to bless us,
but He should be our source of hope, not any other.
This may sound so simple but it can set us free from anger, depression,
hopelessness, confusion, and unnecessary pain.

Let us ask the Lord to forgive us for putting our hope
in people, things, and our abilities.
And let us not be angry with those who disappoint us
because we are as guilty as they are.

Help us God, in Jesus' name.

13

Admit Wrongdoing and Ask Forgiveness

When we admit our wrongdoing,
we take away all Satan's tools and weapons to accuse us.
Admit your wrongdoing and ask for forgiveness as soon as possible,
then talk about the sin and how to avoid it.
There is something so powerful about asking for forgiveness.

Be quick to admit wrongdoing in your marriage,
and be quick to ask for forgiveness.
Help others to repent quickly as well
by creating an opportunity for them to repent and ask for forgiveness.

As Christians, we tell people about the importance of forgiveness.
What about the importance of admitting our wrongdoing?
Evangelism is helping others to repent.
Sometimes people need help to repent.
Let us help each other be quick to repent.

May the Lord give us the ability to ask for forgiveness
and to help others be quick to ask for forgiveness.

14

We Live Out What We Rehearse

If you rehearse something in your mind, it will play out in your mind.
If you rehearse something in your heart, it will play out in your heart.

We think about many things every day.
We think about our spouses, family members, friends, coworkers, finances,
futures, desires, jobs, difficulties, the things we want to do,
the things we don't want to do, etc.

When we begin to think about and rehearse a situation,
we must choose the place of rehearsal.
We can rehearse in our minds or we can rehearse in our hearts.

Perhaps if we always think of someone only in our minds,
when we are around that person our hearts will not be involved.
When we think of someone in our hearts,
our hearts will be engaged when we are around them.

Why should we use our hearts all the time?
The answer is simple:
Our minds can only love conditionally,
but our hearts can love unconditionally.

We cannot truly love with our minds.
If we do, it will be a conditional love.
Only our hearts are capable of loving unconditionally.

Remember, *you will live out what you rehearse.*

15

Gather Love in Your Heart (Part 1)

And you shall love the Lord your God out of and with your whole heart
and out of and with all your soul (your life)
and out of and with all your mind
(with your faculty of thought and your moral understanding)
and out of and with all your strength.
This is the first and principal commandment.
The second is like it and is this, You shall love your neighbor as yourself.
There is no other commandment greater than these

(MARK 12:30-31 AMP).

I give you a new commandment: that you should love one another.
Just as I have loved you, so you too should love one another

(JOHN 13:34 AMP).

Why did Jesus tell us to love like this?

Here are a few things I've found to be true of love:
Love is the highest wealth of all wealth.
Love is the only wealth that we can take to heaven.
Love is the highest power of all powers.
Love is the ultimate medicine.
Love is the only answer to all problems.
Love will unveil the beauty of everything,
even the beauty of this fallen world.
Without love in our hearts we will suffer.
Without love we will be poor inside.
Without love nothing will satisfy.
No power will satisfy but the power of love.
No wealth can satisfy but the wealth of love.
Being around other human beings is very hard and painful
if we are not equipped with the power and wealth of love in our hearts.
Love gives us so much power.
Let us *gather love*.

16

Power Your Heart with Love (Part 2)

Our hearts need to be powered with unconditional love.
Conditional love weakens our hearts.
Conditional love, based on our emotions and reasoning,
fades away just as our emotions and reasoning fade away.
It is shocking to see how often our love for others
is based on our reasoning and our emotions toward them.
The Lord is offering us unconditional love,
but most of us are bound by condition.
The Lord is offering us the highest kind of wealth and power,
but most of us don't show any interest.
If we could really see what He is offering to us,
we would fall to our faces every day to ask Him for more of His love
in our hearts for Him and for others.

There are many problems and only one answer: LOVE.
Ask the Lord to give you more love for Him.
Pick someone and pray for him or her,
asking the Lord to give you true and unconditional love for the person.
Pick a country, pick someone that you don't even like,
pick someone that you've loved based on your own reasoning,
and ask the Lord to drop the power and wealth of love
into your heart toward him or her.

Power your heart.
Power your heart with love!

17

For the Sake of Love

We don't obey the law for the sake of fulfilling the law.
We don't do good things for the sake of being righteous.
We don't pay our taxes because it is the right thing to do.
The law was fulfilled on the cross through Jesus,
and that burden was taken off of mankind's shoulders.

Now we are under a new covenant and a new commandment—love.
Now we obey the law and God's commandments *for the sake of love.*
We pay our taxes without cheating for the sake of love,
not for the sake of doing the right thing.
We live for the sake of love.
We go to our work places for the sake of love.

If we do good things for any reason other than love,
we will become sad, religious people.
Christ serves us with His love.
Have you been served by His love?
He is ever ready to serve us; He is ever ready to love us.
His love never fails.
No matter what we do, He still loves us.
He loves us even when we fall.

18

Homework for Our Hearts

In my school days, I never liked to do my homework.
How about you?
As we all know, homework will usually get students ready for the test.

Are our school days over as adults?
No, life is a school and we are all in it together.
Do we face tests even after we graduate from school and college?
Yes, life is a "school of love" and is filled with tests every single day.
When there is a test there will always be homework,
and as we all know, there will be consequences for not doing our homework.

Where do we do our homework?
The homework will take place in our hearts.
As Jesus mentioned, everything starts in our hearts.

**"but I say to you that everyone who looks at a woman with lust for her
has already committed adultery with her in his heart"**

(MATTHEW 5:28).

Adultery, like any sinful action, will start in our hearts.
Sometimes I find myself doing acts of kindness and being polite toward people.
Now I see that acts of kindness should not be empty actions,
they should come from our hearts.
This is where the homework in our hearts comes in.
How can we do homework in our hearts?
Start meditating in your heart.
Pick someone and picture them through your heart.
Tell them you love them over and over again.
See yourself loving them unconditionally.
After you do this homework in your heart,
there will be a time that you will face the test of loving them unconditionally.
You will pass the test because you did your homework.

How does this process work?
When we meditate on loving someone in our hearts,
we open the door for the love of God to come in.
You can go even higher and see yourself loving
those whom you don't have the smallest reason to like.

You can also do your homework in the area of peace.
Close your eyes and picture yourself receiving peace
from the Prince of Peace, Jesus Christ.
If you do your homework through your heart
and meditate on His peace and the Word of God,
when hard times come as a test, you will pass.

Perhaps we have heard many sermons in our local churches or at conferences.
The only sermons that will stay with us
are the ones that we take into our hearts and meditate on,
the ones that we do our homework on.

The Bible is filled with homework.
When we take God's Word into our hearts,
then we will pass the test when it appears in front of us
and we will be good students in the "school of love."
Have you done your homework in your heart today?
We must not run or escape from our homework anymore.

Everything that is not deeply rooted in our hearts
will be uprooted by the enemy.
If someone gives me a very good fruit tree,
I have to plant it in good ground and water it or it will soon die.
The best place to plant the Word of God,
the best place to do our homework,
the best place to love others and receive peace, joy, and other good fruits
is inside of our hearts.
The more we do our homework in our hearts,
the more ready our hearts will be for the Tree of Life.
The Bible says eternity was planted in our hearts.

He has made everything appropriate in its time.
He has also set eternity in their heart,
yet so that man will not find out the work
which God has done from the beginning even to the end

(ECCLESIASTES 3:11).

Did you do your homework today?
Is your heart ready for the Tree of Life?
The Lord is a gardener.
He loves to plant the Tree of Life in our hearts.
He is offering us His love for the whole world.

What are you feeding your heart?
Did you do your homework, my friend?

I love you even though I don't know you.
I don't know who will read what I am writing now,
but I picture you and I love you in my heart.

Holy Spirit, we repent for not paying better attention
to the homework of love in our hearts.
Forgive us, our Lord.
We rely on You to tutor us.

Let us picture those who are in prison now and have no one to love them.
Let us picture those who are at the hospital and have no visitors.
Let us picture those in Africa that are dying of AIDS and hunger.
Let us make our hearts ready for the Tree of Life.
Let us do the *homework of our hearts*.

19

Maintaining Our Excitement About Jesus

I was so excited when I got to know Jesus Christ.
I was so excited when I gave Him my heart.
My excitement would come out of me
and would affect almost everyone and everything around me.

But somehow in the process of my growth I lost that excitement
and it seemed right in other people's eyes.
They gave me the news that I would lose my excitement over Jesus
as I grew up in my faith.
They told me that I was in a honeymoon stage with Jesus
and it would pass away.

I remember resisting that thought with all my heart,
but somehow it still happened.
As I learned more about His ways, I became less excited about Him.

Is losing our excitement toward Jesus Christ what we call growth?
Nothing should ever steal or overshadow our excitement about Jesus Christ.
No depth of difficulties, no height of success, no fear, no joy,
no lack, no prosperity, no growth, no revelation,
no confusion should ever separate us from being excited
about Jesus Christ, our true excitement and passion.

We should not stop growing or stop being excited over other exciting things.
But we should always put Jesus first and never allow any excitement
to overshadow our excitement toward Jesus Himself.

Apostle Paul kept his excitement over Jesus Christ all his life,
and all his teachings and revelations were about Jesus Christ.
He never separated Jesus' teachings from Jesus Himself,
and as he grew he became more excited about Jesus.
One of the reasons that we lose our excitement and passion toward Jesus
is that we teach about His ways more than about Jesus Himself.

Always put Him first, because He is the Alpha, He is the first, and He should always be first in anything and everything. Putting Him in second or third place is not a good idea at all.

Let Him be first in your life.

Seek to learn this lesson.

Let's ask Him to teach us to always put Him first and in this way *maintain our excitement about Jesus.*

20

The Way We Look at Him

Have you ever been in love?
There is something about looking at someone for the first time
and feeling love and passion for them.
The way we look at each other is so full of fire.
Our faces are radiant.
I remember the way my wife looked at me when we first met.
It was so fulfilling.
I miss that and I know she misses that too.

Do you remember the first time you met Christ?
When we gave our hearts to Him we felt
so much passion toward Him
and we looked at Him with so much love.
Is it possible that He enjoyed our love, passion,
and the way we looked at Him?

I personally believe that He enjoys *the way we look at Him*.
Are we looking at Him the way we used to?
Is He thirsty for our passionate looks?
Absolutely.
What can we do to get back to that place?

Ask Him to stir your heart to look at Him like you did when you first met.
Look at Him in your heart every day like you just met Him for the first time
because He is God and will reveal Himself every day in a new way.
Tell Him every single day that you are glad you met Him.
Think new thoughts toward Him every single day.
Worship Him like you have just discovered Him and been discovered by Him.
Tell Him things you never told Him before.
Walk with Him the way you never walked before.

Touch Him like you never touched Him before.
Be so honest with Him like you have never been before.
Tap into your true feelings for Him and meditate on them.

Look at Jesus for the first time again today.

Christ Is All Revelations Combined Together

Sometimes when we get a revelation from the Lord or we hear a new truth,
we treat that revelation or small truth as God Himself
and we can't stop looking at it.
Our eyes should be fixed on Christ Himself,
not just a revelation that came from Him.
Our food is not revelation but Christ Himself.

We don't treat a piece of the puzzle as the whole picture.
Why should we treat a single revelation or truth as God?

Sometimes we get so caught up in teachings and revelations
that we forget about Jesus our Lord.
He is all revelations and all truths combined together.
He is the whole picture—He is everything.
May we never stop looking at His eyes.
May we never get distracted by a small piece of truth.
Christ is the Truth.

Spending Time with Jesus

There are many ways that we can spend time with Jesus
through studying the Word of God, prayer, etc.

You may say:
"I worked long hours today and didn't have a
chance to spend time with the Lord."
I think our view of spending time with Jesus needs to change a little.

Jesus always sees us, and when we see Him too,
we are spending time with Him.
How can we see Him as we work hard?
We can recognize the fact that He is always with us, in us, and next to us.
Recognizing Jesus is spending time with Him.
Now we don't have any more excuses.
We can spend every second with Jesus by recognizing His presence
as we work, wash the dishes, etc.
Jesus wants to be seen.

Can you imagine if the one you love didn't acknowledge your presence
as you were standing next to them and would only leave a message
or email you?

Leaving messages for Jesus or emailing Him with our prayers is good,
but there is so much more.
He is always with us and wants to be acknowledged.

We love You, Lord, and acknowledge the fact that You are with us.
We see You, Lord.

23

Power to Obey

What will give us the power to obey Jesus?

Our love for Him will give us the power to obey Him.
Gather love in your heart for Jesus.

I used to think if I obeyed Jesus I would be a happy person,
but the fact is that our happiness comes from Jesus and
not from our works for Him.

Let your love for Jesus give you the power to obey Him.
If you try to obey Him without using your deep love for Him,
you will burn yourself out.

Obey Jesus to make Him happy,
but know that your obedience will not make you happy.
Let Jesus be the source of your happiness.
Don't pursue happiness through your obedience.
Your happiness comes from Jesus Himself and not from your works.

We want to obey You because You love us and we love You.
We will be happy just because of You, Jesus Christ.
We will be happy even if we fail.
We will be happy even in our weaknesses.
We will be happy even with our corrupt hearts that are in need of cleansing.
We will be happy even if we can't find our callings.
We will be happy even when we fall
because we know that we will fall into Your arms.
We will be happy because of You, our King.
This will bring the true *power to obey*.

Jesus' Heartbeat

Ask the Holy Spirit to teach you to walk with the *heartbeat of Christ Jesus*.
It is a very important lesson in our Christian walk.
Learn to hear His heartbeat and tune your life with it.
Learn to hear His heartbeat in your own heart,
and to hear and recognize His heartbeat in other people.

Can you hear the call?
His heart is calling; His heart is beating.
Let us march with the heartbeat of Christ.
His heart is beating for all people groups.
His heart is calling.
His heart is calling from other people's hearts that
do not even know Him yet.

It is a mystery, but we can hear and understand some of it.
Let us answer the call and move to His heartbeat.

25

Seeing Jesus in the Flesh

Jesus wants to be seen and recognized in Spirit and in the flesh.
He visited the earth in Spirit and in flesh,
but most people didn't recognize Him and persecuted Him.
He still wants to visit us in the flesh.

The Pharisees were seeking the Messiah but missed
Him when He came to them.
It is easy to recognize the King in kingly clothing,
but it is not easy to recognize Him in ordinary clothing.
The Pharisees were looking for the Messiah to come as a glorious king
who would take all their problems away
and set them free without any cost or struggles.
Does that sound familiar?

They were waiting for a big revival that would make everything
clear and easy.
They missed Him when He was in front of their very eyes;
they even talked to Him and didn't recognize Him.
I am assuming that the high priest could see
the manifest presence of God
at the time of sacrifice and offering,
but missed Him when He appeared as a normal person.

Jesus came 2,000 years ago and chose to live inside of us,
but we are still waiting for Him to come back in a form of revival
that will get everyone saved easily and also give us supernatural love
so that we can automatically love one another.
He will come to us in a form of revival,
but first let us recognize His existence among us
in the flesh and blood of another human being.

He chose to manifest Himself in flesh but we
are still ignoring Him in flesh.
When we only seek Him in Spirit,
we are isolating ourselves from the rest of His body.
He is calling us to see and recognize Him in the flesh.
Let us access the joy of *seeing Jesus in flesh* and blood.
Let us do our parts and He will do His.

**"for I was hungry, and you gave Me nothing to eat;
I was thirsty, and you gave Me nothing to drink"**

(MATTHEW 25:42).

Are we seeking to see Him while He is among us?

Jesus Christ is in Africa without water and most of
us don't recognize His thirst.
He is crying as an orphan and most of us don't hear His cry
because we are only seeking Him in Spirit in our prayer closets.

He is in prison.
He is hungry.
He is calling to be seen and recognized among us.
He is calling to be seen in the flesh.
Let us answer His call.

It Was Jesus All Along

Even when I didn't know God personally, He knew me.
When I didn't have Him in my heart, He had me in His heart.
When I didn't feel His love through Christ,
He gave me His love through the taste of my favorite food,
my favorite toy, and my favorite place.
When I didn't know His beautiful voice, He sang to me through
my favorite song.
When I had no picture of Him in my heart through Christ,
He painted my heart with my favorite things.
When I didn't have Him in Spirit, He came to me in flesh.

He came to me through my family, through movies, clothes, etc.
He was always there.
He uses the people and things around us.

In Africa many are dying,
and the Lord doesn't have as many provisions to work with in the natural.
He doesn't have many people who are willing to help the
needy and dying.
But the Lord can use anything around those people to show His love to them.

The Lord is always ready to show Himself to people,
but He uses us to minister to each other.
If He didn't, hungry people in Africa would be showered
by food from the sky.

Before I had the Holy Spirit in my heart,
the Lord came to me through the natural things of this world,
such as food or the hugs and love of another human being.

Since I gave my heart to the Lord,
He comes to me through those things and

also through His Holy Spirit in my heart.
Even if I don't eat good food, or if no one loves me,
I have His direct love in my heart.

But for those who don't know Him in the Spirit,
He will usually love them through what is around them physically.
That is why it is very important to allow God to pour His love through us
to those who have never been introduced to Him and His Spirit.

Even if we don't tell those people about God,
He wants to love them through our acts of giving.
One day those people will see who is behind our giving and love.

It took the Lord thirty-three years to show me that He was behind
my favorite things.
He was behind the dark chocolate that I always loved.
He was behind my grandmother's love.
He was behind my mother, my brother and sisters, my father.
It was Jesus all along, but He was not hasty to show that it was Him.
He simply allowed me to taste some of Himself
and He came to me on January 21, 2000.

He is still revealing His love to me more and more.
Now He is not just Spirit, He is everywhere and in everything I love.
He is even in my fireplace and behind my favorite movie.

I love You, God.
I am in love with You.

"I am so in love with you too," He says to all of us.

27

Strong Hearts and Minds

We need strength, focus, boldness, and toughness
in order to carry out our callings
and God's commandments on earth.
Christ was a very strong-minded person.
He was not weak toward others.
He was very bold and was not easily moved by anything but His Father.
If He was not a strong man,
He couldn't have carried out His Father's commandments.
He may not have been very strong physically
but He was strong in mind and heart.

What was the root of Jesus' strength and toughness?
The answer is love.

Love was and is the root of His strength and toughness.
Let us be strong, but still receive our strength and toughness from godly love.
We need to be strong, focused, and bold so that we can spread God's love.
Some may think that weakness in heart and mind will carry God's love,
but I believe *strength in heart and mind will carry His love.*

The disciples could not have done what they did
if they were not strong, focused, and tough.
But they all got their strength, focus, and toughness
from the love of the Father.
May His love make us strong so that we can carry it around.

28

Wrestling with God

Why should we wrestle with God?
Have you seen a lion wrestling with his cub?
Will wrestling help the cub grow stronger?

Our Father in heaven is the Lion.
Satan wants to be a lion and he tries to act and roar like one.
He always wanted to be like God.

I believe wrestling with the true Lion, our Father in heaven,
helps us face Satan and his foes and not be shaken.

How can we wrestle with God?
Start by asking Him to wrestle with you first.
One way to wrestle with the Lord is to knock persistently.

**Then He said to them,
"Suppose one of you has a friend,
and goes to him at midnight and says to him,
'Friend, lend me three loaves;
for a friend of mine has come to me from a journey,
and I have nothing to set before him';
and from inside he answers and says,
'Do not bother me;
the door has already been shut and my children and I are in bed;
I cannot get up and give you anything.'
"I tell you, even though he will not get up
and give him anything because he is his friend,
yet because of his persistence he will get up
and give him as much as he needs"**

(LUKE 11:5-8).

We can also *wrestle with the Lord by being extremely honest*
about our true feelings and even our disappointments.

What if He started to provoke you to wrestle with Him long ago
but you refused because it was not a holy act to you?
I believe the true Lion, our Father, is always ready
to wrestle with His cubs (us).

Get ready to wrestle.
If Jacob did it, we can do it.
If the Lord wrestled with Jacob, He will wrestle with us.
It will be fun and it might hurt a little.
The pain of wrestling with our Father is an honor
that will give us enough authority to face Satan, the artificial lion.

Are you ready for the call?

29

Facing Lions

Imagine you have a very powerful gun in your hand
and are *facing a lion* that is getting ready to charge you.
You would be thankful for the gun, but is that all you need to face the lion?
What will happen if your hands start to shake?

My fellow brothers and sisters, exercise your God-given authority.
Point your weapons toward the lion that is seeking
to devour you, and stop shaking.

**Be of sober spirit, be on the alert.
Your adversary, the devil, prowls about like a roaring lion,
seeking someone to devour**

(I PETER 5:8).

Christianity is not just about being nice, meek, and naive.
There is a time to be a lamb and there is a time to be a lion.
Most of us know how to be lambs,
now let us ask God the Father to teach us how to be lions.

We are children of the Lion and the Lamb.
It is a very strange combination.

He wants us to be wise as serpents and gentle as doves (see Matthew 10:16).
That is a strange combination also.
May your hands never shake as you face the enemy.
May God impart boldness and courage into your heart day and night.
May you face the lion with the proper weapons
and God-given courage.

Are you ready?
The Lord is calling.
Let's go face some lions.

The Face of the Enemy

The worldly mindset will advise us to study our enemies
in order to bring them down.
In the kingdom of God we don't study our enemies,
we bring them down with the name above all other names,
Christ Jesus our Lord.
David didn't study or meditate on the height of Goliath,
he just defeated him.

You are not called to meditate and look upon your problem for a long time.
You don't have to be tall and strong like your problem in order to defeat it.
If you were as strong and tall as your problems,
when you defeated them the credit would go to you and not to the Lord.
Your height and strength would be lifted up and exalted.
When you are small and weak, the glory will go to the Lord.
When you are small and weak,
you are eligible to face the enemy and build an everlasting testimony.

As you face your enemy, don't meditate on his height, face, or strength.
If you do it will bring you down.
You have Christ in you.
You can stop meditating on the enemy.
You can stop shaking.
We are called to be as wise as serpents (see Matthew 10:16).
True wisdom will help us to see the face of our Lord
and *meditate on His face and height, not the face and height of our enemies.*
No matter how tall, how wide, or how strong our enemy,
the Lord is the tallest, strongest, and most beautiful of all.
The Lord is the Beginning and the End (see Revelation 22:13).

We can do it.
We can look upon His face rather than our enemies' faces.
It is so much more fun looking at Jesus' face as we go toward our enemies.

Now, after learning to stop looking at the size of our enemies,
it is also time to stop looking at our own size.
We can apply the same principle here.
Meditate on the Lord God Almighty.

31

We Cannot But He Can

Moses said he could not deliver the Israelites out of Egypt
like the Lord asked him to,
and the anger of the Lord burned against him (see Exodus 4:10-14).
What really made the Lord angry?

The Lord didn't get angry because of what Moses said.
He got angry at what Moses didn't say.
I think it is very important to acknowledge our powerlessness,
but it is more important to acknowledge the Lord's might and power.
We can do nothing on our own, but we can do all things through Him.
Moses was right about his condition,
but he didn't see and acknowledge the Lord's might, power,
and ability to accomplish the task.

It may take some of us forty years to acknowledge
that we can do nothing in our own power,
and another forty years to see the Lord's might and power
and to know that we can do all things through Him.

Lord, let us not walk around the wilderness twenty, forty, or eighty years.
Help us to learn this now.
Help us with our unbelief.

Lord, we can do nothing in our own strength and power,
but we can do all things through You.
Help us to get this revelation and be so needy toward You.
Help us to acknowledge our neediness toward You in every situation,
and to believe in You and Your might.
We cannot but you can.

In Your beautiful name, Amen.

The Only One Who Deserves Our Fear Is Almighty God

When I was a Muslim,
I gave the god of Islam so much respect without even knowing him.
Now that I have a relationship with the true God,
I don't give Him the respect that is due to Him.
I get too casual with Jesus Christ sometimes.

True fear, awe, and respect toward God Almighty
provide a very strong covering for us.
Godly fear will bring security and will cause us to rest in awe
that He is mighty and great and above all things.
Godly fear protects us and is needed in our love relationship with Him.

How I wish that I could know His fear and rest in it.
Grant me Your fear, O Lord, that I may praise You with awe.

The only fear that brings rest is the holy fear of God.
Do you want to rest?
Sometimes we submit to any fear but the fear of God.
This can be the cause of our restlessness.

We should know that *the only One who deserves our fear is Almighty God.*
No other person or thing deserves our fear.

I don't want to be afraid of You, but I want to have
Your fear in me, Almighty God.
Teach me how to mix Your fear with Your love
and never separate those two from each other.

As we grow in the fear of God, the enemy has less access to our lives.
We can burn every other fear with the holy fear of the
one true God in our hearts.

The Bible says that perfect love will cast out all fear:

There is no fear in love; but perfect love casts out fear,
because fear involves punishment, and the one who fears
is not perfected in love

(I JOHN 4:18).

This is not referring to the holy fear of God.
When we mix the love of God with His holy fear,
it will cause grace to abound in our lives.

And He will delight in the fear of the Lord,
And He will not judge by what His eyes see,
Nor make a decision by what His ears hear

(ISAIAH 11:3).

And He will be the stability of your times,
A wealth of salvation, wisdom and knowledge;
The fear of the Lord is his treasure

(ISAIAH 33:6).

So the church throughout all Judea and Galilee
and Samaria enjoyed peace, being built up;
and going on in the fear of the Lord and in the comfort of the Holy Spirit,
it continued to increase

(ACTS 9:31).

33

He Is Never Late

One night I was so discouraged when I looked at our bank account online.
I started to talk to the Lord and this is what came out of my heart:

Lord, why are You always late?
I know that You always provide for us, but why are
You late most of the time?
You were late in the desert with the Israelites
and that caused them to rebel against You.
Why are You always late in our lives?

Should I stop full-time ministry, forget about my calling,
and go get a normal job?
I know You called me into this, but why are You late all the time?
Why do we always have to be short?

All of a sudden the life was taken out of me.
I could not move; I had no life in me.
It was a very strange and empty feeling.
We are used to having life in us all the time,
and it is very strange when the life is taken out of us
even for a very short moment.

I felt that the Lord gave me the option of snapping out of it and coming back.
I pulled myself out of it and came back to life.
Then I felt the Lord say:
"If I was late, you would be dead."

I realized what a precious gift it is to have life in me.
I never appreciated the life that the Lord gave me.
He gave His life so that I may carry life.
He died that I may live.
He is never late.

He is always on time.
If He was late, we would all be dead.

Then for the money issue, He reminded me of what Judas did to Him.
Judas betrayed Christ for money.
Maybe he needed that money.
Maybe he was under some kind of financial pressure.
I don't think he hated Jesus and wanted Him dead.
He may have been greedy or desperate for money and it led to Jesus' betrayal.

I told the Lord how sorry I was for entertaining the thought
of betraying Him for the lack of money.
Denying Christ like Peter did is one thing,
but betraying Him like Judas is another matter.

May we never back down from our callings because of our lack or needs.
May we never betray the Son of God for money.
May we live in *His* timing with courage, patience, and faith in Him.

We love You, wonderful Son of God.
Thank You from the depths of our hearts for opening our eyes.

We love You, Lovely One.
Get us on Your time.

From Getting to Giving

I had a meeting with a minister today and it was very hard for me.
When I got back home, I asked the Lord to tell me the reason.
I felt He said that I went to the meeting to receive, not to give.
I went to the meeting to get some possible connection for future ministry.

May the Lord change our attitude from getting to giving.
Selfishness will creep in on us and jump on our shoulders.
No matter what we do, if we do it to gain something,
we will never be satisfied.

Most of our giving is conditional,
and conditional acts open the door for our old nature to kick in.
Unconditional acts open the door for our new nature to come in.
When our new nature rules, there is peace and comfort in the Spirit.
But when our old nature rules, there is agony and discomfort.

May we allow the Spirit of God to come out of us
through our unconditional acts and thoughts.

35

The Connection Between Faith and Desire

I believe the strength of our desires (passion) will greatly
affect the level of our faith.
The strength of our faith will carry us into the promised land of God.
Sometimes in the past I have asked the Lord for greater faith
in order to enter into the promised land.
Now I see that I should ask Him to increase the desire of my heart first,
and that will open the door for stronger faith to come into my heart.

We can examine the strength of our desires and passion in our own hearts.
Pick a desire and see on a scale of one to ten what the strength of your desire is.
As our desires grow stronger, more faith will be deposited into our hearts.

How strong is your desire to be free?
To spread God's love?
To love God in a romantic way?
To trust Him in all things?
To love others to the degree of laying your life down for them?
To be financially stable?
To have a godly marriage?
To fulfill your calling?
To enter into God's promises for your life?
To see the right president in office?
To feed the poor and comfort the brokenhearted?

Holy Spirit, we give You full permission
to give us any desire You want our hearts to carry.
We want to have extreme passion for what You desire.
Make our hearts pregnant with Your desires.

May the Holy Spirit of God give us stronger desires and passion
for God's plan for our lives and the faith to walk them out.

36

Pretending Will Make Us Blind to the Truth

Have you ever pretended not to see something that was
right in front of your eyes?
Have you ever closed your eyes to something?
Closing our eyes to the truth will lead to blindness toward the truth.
There are truths about ourselves that we close our eyes to.
There are also wrong things going on in front of our eyes that
we pretend not to see.
The Lord came to the Pharisees as a form of truth,
but they chose to close their eyes and pretend they didn't see any truth in Him
because the truth He brought was confrontational.
In the Book of Matthew, Jesus talks about a group of people
whom God blinded so that they would not see the truth.

And the disciples came and said to Him,
"Why do You speak to them in parables?"
And He answered and said to them,
"To you it has been granted to know the mysteries of the kingdom of heaven,
but to them it has not been granted.

"For whoever has, to him more shall be given, and he shall have an abundance;
but whoever does not have, even what he has shall be taken away from him.

"Therefore I speak to them in parables;
because while seeing they do not see,
and while hearing they do not hear, nor do they understand.

"And in their case the prophecy of Isaiah is being fulfilled, which says,
'You will keep on hearing, but will not understand;
And you will keep on seeing, but will not perceive;
'For the heart of this people has become dull,
And with their ears they scarcely hear,
And they have closed their eyes

Lest they should see with their eyes,
And hear with their ears,
And understand with their heart and return,
And I should heal them'"

(MATTHEW 13:10-15).

I always wondered why.
Now I know one reason is that they chose to close their eyes to the truth
for so long that it led them into permanent blindness.
Of course with the Lord anything is possible and
He can remove their blindness,
but we should be careful to always welcome the truth when it appears to us.
No matter how hard and confrontational it gets,
we must never close our eyes to it and never pretend we haven't seen it.
Now is the time to ask the Holy Spirit to search our hearts
and find those areas in which we have been blinded toward the truth
so we can ask for forgiveness from the Lord.
He is so forgiving and ready to give our sight back.

Let us welcome Him as the Truth in our lives.

37

Bound by Good

We can be bound in a very negative way by good
if we don't seek and choose to see the truth.
The Pharisees often offended Jesus with their good deeds,
but the truth has never offended our Lord.

The Pharisees rested on the Sabbath day.
When Jesus healed someone on the Sabbath,
it made them angry and offended them, and they totally missed the truth.
The Pharisees were obeying the law, doing what they thought was good,
but they became bound by the law and what they called good things.

Has the Son of God ever offended us by revealing the truth to us?
Have the law and good things ever bound us, causing
us to offend the Son of God?

The truth is, we can be bound by good in a negative way
if we don't seek, see, and bring the truth.
We are not followers of good, but seekers and embracers of truth.
Truth is perfect, good is not.
We don't want to be bound by good; we want to be set free by truth.

**For the Law was given through Moses;
grace and truth were realized through Jesus Christ**

(JOHN 1:17).

Ask the Lord to forgive you for following good rather than truth.
Ask Him to forgive you for judging others
according to right or wrong rather than the truth.
Ask Him to stop you from going to the tree of knowledge of good and evil,
and start going to the Tree of Life instead.

Always choose the Tree of Life.

Never be offended by Jesus showing grace to those whom we call sinners.

May the Lord set us free from good, and lead us to the truth.

In His beautiful and perfect name, Amen.

Our Wrongdoing Thermometers

I was mad at my wife today and was mean to her over the phone.
When I get angry with her, my heart hurts afterward.
I don't want to ever hurt her heart.
It hurts me to hurt her.
It is not something that happens every day,
but it happens sometimes in every marriage.
What I did today was wrong, and I knew it.

I went before the Lord in prayer and asked Him why
He allowed me to hurt her.
Why didn't He help me to be nice to her?
I told Him that I don't want to hurt anyone.

I felt the Lord answer me in my heart that she is
not the only one I hurt today—
there are others.
In a moment I realized how I hurt others without even knowing them.

Let me explain.
What would happen if people in places of authority
decided not to show up to their jobs?
What would happen if an ambulance driver, doctor, nurse, or even a cab driver
did not show up or take their job seriously?
How many people would get hurt?
When I don't do my job, I am hurting people without knowing it.
As carriers of God's Spirit on earth, we have jobs to do.
Our job is to love.
We have been given authority to set the captives free.
We have been given the Comforter to comfort those who are heavily burdened.
We have a message of freedom and eternal life that should be spread.
We have been given spiritual medicine for the sick and needy.

We have been given access to the God of the universe
and should help others to have the same access.

Being nice people or being careful that we
don't hurt anyone is not our only goal.
It is not just about checking the *thermometer*
of our wrongdoing every day.
Even if we don't hurt anyone through wrongdoing,
we are hurting many when we don't do our God-given jobs.
We simply hurt many people when we don't put
to work the talents the Lord gave us.
Many of us are so concerned with watching the thermometer
of our wrongdoing
that it is all we do all day long.

Many of us have kept the records of our wrongdoing very well.
In some cases we might go to those whom we wronged and ask for forgiveness.
In other cases we might just go to the Lord for forgiveness.

The Lord gave us jobs to do, but many of us are not only late,
but never showed up in the first place.
What about people we never met but still hurt with our lack of responsibility?
How many people have I wronged by not telling them about Christ?
Am I accountable for that kind of wrongdoing?
I have no idea how many people I have hurt by not showing up
on the job the Lord gave me.

Today I realized that I am far guiltier than I could imagine.
It was not just my wife whom I hurt.
Only God knows how many others were hurt by me today.
May the Lord forgive me for hurting so many people.

People are hurting because Satan has many who do his jobs
and take them very seriously.
People in the pornography, drug, and alcohol industries
are taking their jobs very seriously.

Let us take our jobs seriously.
Let us focus not so much on what we might be doing wrong
but what we can do right that will bring a ripple effect of
love and truth into the world.

With the help of technology, TV, and the Internet,
we can comfort, help, and give medicine to the multitudes.
I am not trying to bring shame or fear to myself or to you,
I am trying to allow our hearts to see the truth
about the importance of our callings and jobs on earth.

The Lord is calling us.
Let us answer His call.

39

Seeing Past Our Mistakes

Every day I make mistakes.
No matter what I do, when I look back, I will see some kind of mistake.
Am I going to stop growing in Christ?
No.
Am I always going to see my past mistakes?
Yes.
Should I stop doing what I do?
Absolutely not.

What should we do then?
We must keep doing our best, and know that we are not perfect.
As we grow in Him we will see more of our mistakes.

It is funny how we look into our pasts and recognize our mistakes
and then somehow believe what we are doing now is not a mistake.
We think we know what to do now.

As we grow in Him, we will see that our current actions
are not as perfect and right as we thought they would be.

Why am I telling you this?
I want us to see that we all make mistakes,
and what we do is never going to be perfect.
The closer we get to Christ's perfection,
the more what we do will seem imperfect.

God is not concerned about your perfection.
Do your best, attach yourself to Him and His perfection,
and know you will never do any perfect act on your own.

Walk toward Him and don't be embarrassed
by your past decisions and mistakes,

and don't be so proud of your present decisions and actions.
It is normal for our past to seem full of mistakes as we walk toward Him.
We are growing in God and every day our eyes will be more open
and our pasts will seem more imperfect.
We want to stop seeing our past mistakes and start seeing past our mistakes.

Just keep moving.
He loves you so much.
Keep looking into His beautiful eyes of love and acceptance.

40

Our Decisions Will Affect Others

Our decisions about others can bring pain or comfort into their lives.
*Our decisions about our own lives can
also greatly affect other people's lives.*
We have the power to affect each other.
We are all connected.

The Lord is reigning in heaven, but He gave
the earth into the hands of men.

**The heavens are the heavens of the LORD;
But the earth He has given to the sons of men**

(PSALM 115:16).

He also gave us free will.
I want to consider others and know that my decisions about my own life
will also affect them.
We are not here for our own benefit but for God's plan and purposes.
We are not called to make decisions based on the
benefit they will bring for us.

Ask yourself some questions before you make a decision.
How will this decision affect other people's lives?
Am I here just for me?

Please know that your decisions will affect other people.
Consider others when you make decisions.

41

Perfect Decisions

Sometimes we can't make a decision.
We stay in confusion and fear because none of our options are perfect.

Sometimes we don't have many options to choose from,
like King David when he ate the forbidden bread in the temple
(see I Samuel 21).
If we wait for perfect options, we might miss what is in front of us.
King David chose the best option that was put in front of him by the Lord,
and his decision was not perfect in many people's eyes.
The enemy has held back many of us with
the fear of making an imperfect decision
and has kept us in the prison of fear and confusion.

Fear of making imperfect decisions will stop us
from making any decisions at all.
This can really keep us from moving forward
in our relationships, jobs, callings, etc.

Let us check our hearts and pick the best option
that the Lord puts in front of us and get out of confusion in Jesus' name.
The Pharisees were trying so hard to make a perfect decision
that they missed the only perfect One ever made.
Let us ask the Lord to forgive us for judging people
who made imperfect decisions according to the
choices that were set before them.
We are not trying to make perfect decisions,
but to pick the best option that is set before us by the Lord
and trust we are in His perfect will for our lives.
He always gives us choices.
And He loves us always.

42

Is Obeying the Law Easier Than Facing the Truth?

It is very important to choose to see and
embrace the truth in every situation.
The Pharisees were seekers of the truth in some cases,
but not embracers of the truth.
They sought the Messiah, but when He came they didn't embrace Him
because the truth was too costly to face.
Obeying the law was much easier than facing the truth.
They chose to blind themselves to the truth, and ultimately kill the truth,
following the law instead.
*It is very important to look at everything through
the eyes of truth rather than the law.*

What is the truth anyway?
Is it what we think it is?
What is the truth about people who lack the ability to love?
Are they bad people, or have they never been loved?
What is the truth about unsaved people?
Do they not want Jesus, or have they never been
introduced to the real Jesus?
What is the truth about those who kill?
Are they bad people, or could they have been
abused, molested, or hurt in the past?
What is the truth about Muslim suicide bombers?
Do they kill because they enjoy killing,
or could they have been deceived and misinformed?
What is the truth about homeless people who ask for food or money?
Are they all the same?

It is so easy to categorize everything, including people.
And it's so easy to judge according to the law of good and evil,
but it is not easy to seek the truth and embrace it.
Let us ask the Lord to help us see
and embrace the truth, in His beautiful name.

43

Being a Good Person

The rich young ruler called Jesus a good master and His response was,

"Why do you call Me good? No one is good except God alone"

(SEE LUKE 18:19).

Of course the rich young ruler didn't see who Jesus really was.
He called a human being a good master, and Jesus questioned him.

Now the questions we should ask are:
Am I a good person?
What will make me a good person?
Am I a better person than a murderer?
Are my sins lighter than the sins of others?
Whose sin is greater, a person who was caught in the act of adultery,
or a person who is committing adultery in his or her heart?

Should we call ourselves better people than adulterers
because we've never physically been
unfaithful to our wives or husbands?
Who says we are better than the Muslims who
bomb buildings and kill people?
Should we call ourselves better people because
we've never physically killed anyone?
We are all sinners.

Who is the biggest sinner?
Paul said he was (see I Timothy 1:15).
The only One who is good is God.
We become good through the blood of Jesus Christ.

Forgive us, Lord, for thinking that we are better than other people.
Our ability to hear God's voice does not make us better

than those who don't have a relationship with God.
As Christians we should put down our pride
and know that we are not better than those whom we call unsaved.
We are all sinners and we all need Jesus' forgiveness every day.
It is about Jesus, not about our goodness.
May the Lord help us to see one another as He sees us,
and may He help us to love one another as He loves.

44

Laying Down Our Crowns

When we have crowns on our heads,
it is hard to bow down to the One who gave them to us.
We stand up straight in order to keep
our crowns on our heads,
but if we are going to bow down,
we must lay aside our crowns.
How can we bow down to the Lord if
we have crowns on our heads?

Many crowns will be offered to us from believers, unbelievers, and even God,
but we are called to lay them down constantly.
Never keep your crown on your head.
If you do, then you cannot bow down to the One who gave it to you.

And when the living creatures give glory and honor and thanks
to Him who sits on the throne, to Him who lives forever and ever,
the twenty-four elders will fall down before Him who sits on the throne,
and will worship Him who lives forever and ever,
and will cast their crowns before the throne, saying,

"Worthy are You, our Lord and our God, to receive glory and honor and power; for You
created all things, and because of Your will they existed, and were created"

(REVELATION 4:9-11).

Let us not to be concerned about our crowns on earth.
Even in heaven we are going to lay down our crowns to bow to Christ.
May the Lord forgive us for keeping our crowns on our heads.

45

Preach to Heaven and Let the Earth Hear

I used to talk to heaven about Jesus as I spoke before an audience,
but at some point I allowed the atmosphere and variety of my audiences
to affect me and cause me to talk to them instead.

Why not let heaven be your audience?
Look at Jesus and your audience will see Him through your eyes.
Preach to heaven and let the earth hear your message.
Sing to heaven and let the earth hear it from heaven.
Send everything above and let it rain down on your audience.
Talk to heaven, sing songs to heaven,
and tell heaven how you feel about God.

46

Expanding God's Kingdom

This morning I asked the Lord, "Why do you want me to always forgive?
Is it because You want me to be a good person?"

This is what I heard in my heart:
"Every time you forgive, you open the door for My kingdom
to come in and be expanded on earth."

I realized that our calling is not about us,
it is about His kingdom being established and
expanded on earth as it is in heaven.
Our focus should not be on establishing our own kingdoms and ministries.
Every kingdom but His kingdom is subject to failure.
We don't want to promote ourselves with our gifts, we want to preach Jesus.
We don't want to expand our kingdoms; we want to expand God's kingdom.

May we all build and establish His kingdom
through love, forgiveness, healing, deliverance, encouragement,
peace, joy, laughter, giving, prayer, intercession, etc.

When the body of Christ concentrates on building His kingdom,
we will be filled with joy when we hear that someone else is
successful in ministry, whether it is a church, home group, outreach, or
healing ministry.
Our goal is to manifest His kingdom and heal people,
no matter whom it manifests through.

If you are a musician, you will be happy if
someone else makes a very anointed CD.
If you are a preacher, you will be happy if someone
preaches an anointed sermon, because the kingdom of our
Father was manifested or expanded through their preaching.

If someone gets healed or is raised from
the dead through someone else's prayer,
you will still be happy that the kingdom of our Father touched the earth.
We should not be jealous when God moves through others.

The world is in desperate need of the establishment of God's kingdom.
Let us answer the call.
We can't do it alone; we need to do it together.
Let us build His kingdom.

**Your kingdom come.
Your will be done on earth as it is in heaven**

(MATTHEW 6:10 AMP).

The King wants to expand His kingdom.

47

Kingdom Keys

"I will give you the keys of the kingdom of heaven;
and whatever you shall bind on earth shall be bound in heaven,
and whatever you shall loose on earth shall be loosed in heaven"

(MATTHEW 16:19).

The Lord Jesus wants to put the keys of the kingdom of heaven
in our hearts instead of in our hands.
If we receive the kingdom keys in our hands,
we will use them to expand our own kingdoms and not His.
*But if we receive the kingdom keys in our hearts,
we will use them to expand His kingdom.*
Is your heart ready to receive the keys?
Holy Spirit, make our hearts ready for the keys of the kingdom.

48

Preaching Christ

When you talk about the King, talk as if He is alive, because He is.
He is much more alive than we are.

When I was a new Christian, Christ was much
more alive to me than He is now.
Christ doesn't change.
He is always alive.
What happened then?

Somehow I began preaching myself rather than preaching Christ.
I used the gifts and knowledge of Christ in me to
show others how alive I was.
Preaching self will drain life from us, *but preaching
Christ will fill us with life*.
The more we preach Him, the more life will flow through and out of us.

If we preach ourselves, when people reject us it will make us angry.
If we preach Christ, we will not be angry at all when people reject us.

Christ is alive.
Christ is near.
Christ is here.

Rise up our King and take Your place in us.
We abide in You so that others may see You, not us.

And when I came to you, brethren,
I did not come with superiority of speech or of wisdom,
proclaiming to you the testimony of God.

For I determined to know nothing among you except Jesus Christ,
and Him crucified.

And I was with you in weakness and in fear and in much trembling.

And my message and my preaching were not in persuasive words of wisdom,
but in demonstration of the Spirit and of power,
that your faith should not rest on the wisdom of men, but on the power of God

(I CORINTHIANS 2:1-5).

49

Life Is in the Manger

**And she gave birth to her first-born son;
and she wrapped Him in cloths, and laid Him in a manger,
because there was no room for them in the inn**

(LUKE 2:7).

It sometimes seems that what is important to God is not important to us,
and what is important to us is not important to Him.
Could it be that what appears insignificant in
our eyes is very significant in His eyes?
Jesus hides behind the little things we think are insignificant,
but most often we look for Him in the big happenings.

The Pharisees did not recognize Jesus when He came
because He was not big enough.
He came as a carpenter's son.
He was only thirty years old and did not have a proper education
through the synagogue.
He was born in a stable and placed in a manger,
which is a long, open box or trough that horses or cattle eat from.

The Pharisees were waiting for the Messiah to appear as a mighty king,
but Christ appeared so normal.
There was no room in any inn for the King of
all mankind to enter the world in.
God planned this from the beginning
to show us the importance of the seemingly insignificant.
The Source of Life was found in a manger.
He was manifested there in that insignificant place.
He *chose* that place.
All too often we look for the Life in the mansions of our minds.

Fear will categorize our lives and tell us what is important and what is not.
Fear will always tell us to go after big things and leave the small behind.
Fear will tell us to hurry and get the seemingly important things done first.
Fear will cause us to rush and miss the value of small things.
Fear will compel us to want to be around those
whom we think are more important
and leave the less important people behind.

Who is really more important than whom?
In many of the visions of modern day prophets,
such as Rick Joyner and Bob Jones,
the most important people are seemingly insignificant people,
such as beggars who had only a small amount of love to give.
But it was not small to God.

Fear will blind us from seeing small things.
But guess what?
God is mostly in small things.
For some reason He manifests Himself through people
and things that we think are meaningless.
Some of us think our jobs are not important.
What if we start to think our jobs are the most important things
on this planet in God's eyes?
If we put all of our hearts and souls into
the jobs God has given us right now
and consider them important, we will see God in them every day.

You see, fear will always keep us from enjoying the simple things in life.
Fear will keep us from seeing the Life inside the manger.
There is such a peace and joy when
the Lord opens our eyes and gives us the gift
of seeing and enjoying the simple things of this world.
May the Lord open our eyes to the Life inside the manger of His love.
There is love in the manger.
What mangers have we missed in our lives?
Where is our Messiah?
Are we looking in the right places?

He can be found in a very simple conversation with our neighbor's children,
a homeless person or beggar, a friend who is grieving,
the sick and the needy, or an old friend.
He can be seen in the person right in front of you.
Make that person the center of your attention.
That person has so much value in the eyes of the Lord.

Start watching.
Focus on the moment and where Jesus is,
what He is doing, what He *looks* like.
He can be heard in the sound of a frying egg on the stove.
Make that sound the center of your attention.
Start listening.
Focus on what He *sounds* like.
Where is our Messiah?
He is everywhere.
Suddenly, everything in your day becomes significant.

Lord, forgive us for ignoring the beautiful, simple things of this life.
Forgive us for rejecting You when
You came in a way that was insignificant to us.
Lord, open our eyes that we may see You in the mangers of life all around us.

50

Jesus' Wedding Day

Have you ever seen a wedding being planned?
It involves many different people working as a team
and a wedding coordinator who puts the whole thing together.

As we know, our Lord is planning to get married
and He will have a marriage ceremony sooner or later.
Many angels are working to prepare His wedding.
Are we helping them prepare for the ceremony?
Have we sent the invitation that we carry in our hearts
to others who don't know about the wedding?

It is an honor to be part of the Son of God's wedding.
Not only are we all invited to the wedding,
but we are all invited to help with the preparations.
Let us work hard to prepare His wedding ceremony.
Let us be in unity with the Holy Spirit (the coordinator),
with the angels, and with each other.
We have a wedding to plan.

Help us beautiful Son of God to plan Your wedding.
We love You so much and are excited to plan Your wedding
and to see Your wedding day.
Forgive us for paying so much attention to ourselves
and for forgetting about Your wedding.
I am so excited, my friend Jesus.
I am excited for Your marriage.
I love You so much.
I care about You, my love.
You are so wonderful, our King.

51

On Our Knees

Being filled with the Holy Spirit of God is a free gift through Jesus,
but getting connected to the Holy Spirit inside of
us involves action on our part.
Many of us have the Holy Spirit of God inside,
but few of us are connected to Him on a daily basis.

I asked the Holy Spirit to tell me how I could get
connected to Him inside of me.
I heard Him say, "on your knees."
Getting down on our knees shows our neediness
and respect toward the Holy Spirit of God.
Getting on our knees in front of others is so humbling.
Being on our knees will not make us more holy—
it is the sign of neediness.
Our holiness will not attract the Holy Spirit of God,
but our neediness will.

52

Opening the Door for the Holy Spirit

I do not believe that fasting makes us more holy.
It is a physical act that *opens the door for the Holy Spirit to come in.*
Prayer is another physical act that opens the
door for the Spirit of God to move.
Ask the Holy Spirit to show you how to open the door for Him.

Fasting and praying will prepare the way
for the Holy Spirit of God to manifest in us and through us.
I used to think if I would fast, I would become more holy.
Now I know that when I fast, I open the door for
the Holy One to come in.
There is a big difference between becoming holy
and opening the door for the Holy One to rush
out of us into this world.

We do not need to focus on becoming more holy—
we are holy through the Son of God;
we need to simply open the door for the Holy One to come in.

53

Playing by His Rules

When people play sports, they have to play
by certain rules and regulations.
We don't make fun of them for playing by a set rules.
Athletes are not mocked for moving the way they do.

Basketball players and football players have fun as they play;
that sport is their hobby.
There is nothing wrong with having hobbies.

When we play with the Holy Spirit of God,
we have to *play by His rules*, and He changes His rules all the time.

We see people in some churches who move in a strange way.
Sometimes they look funny.
Should we judge them for the way they move?
No.
Should we judge athletes for the way they move
when they play sports?
No.
Does the Holy Spirit want to play with His children?
Yes.
Does He have His own rules that change all the time?
Yes.

Why does He always change?
Because He is unlimited and full of creativity.
Does He want us to be creative and let go and follow His creativity?
Yes.
Have fun with the Holy Spirit.

54

Affected and Moved by Needs and News

Do you ever find yourself being moved by news that you hear
and by people's requests and needs?

Now a certain man was sick, Lazarus of Bethany,
the village of Mary and her sister Martha.

And it was the Mary who anointed the Lord with ointment,
and wiped His feet with her hair, whose brother Lazarus was sick.

The sisters therefore sent to Him, saying, "Lord, behold, he whom You love is sick."

But when Jesus heard it, He said,
"This sickness is not unto death, but for the glory of God,
that the Son of God may be glorified by it."

Now Jesus loved Martha, and her sister, and Lazarus.

When therefore He heard that he was sick,
He then stayed two days longer in the place where He was.

Then after this He said to the disciples, "Let us go to Judea again."

The disciples said to Him,
"Rabbi, the Jews were just now seeking to stone You,
and are You going there again?"

(JOHN 11:1-8)

Jesus was not affected by His friend's need for healing
or His enemies' plans for killing Him.
Let us take a look at our own lives and see what affects us.
Jesus was not affected by His friendship with Lazarus, Mary, and Martha.

He was not affected by the fact that the Jews were seeking to stone Him.
He was moved by His Father.

How much does the news we hear affect our prayers and our lives?
Does what we hear and see cause us to react out of need and fear?

Sometimes we get so caught up in the news on TV
that we forget how powerful and mighty our God is.
Sometimes we work to take care of people's needs and wants.
Others' will in our lives can cause God's will in our lives to fade.

When we live for the King of all kings,
nothing should affect us but the King and His will.
The King sees what we can't see; He has all of our interests at heart.

Nothing should affect us and move us more than Him—
not our feelings, failures, news we hear, people's approval or disapproval,
control, manipulation, lack,
plenty, sickness, health, friendship, etc.

When we get to the place of being affected
and moved by the Holy Spirit,
we can truly love people, not just please them.
In that stage the fear of man will be burned up
and the fear of the Lord will accompany us.
Some people around us may start to manifest, judge us,
and get very angry at our decisions.
People may call us rude, insensitive, and even proud.
Others may persecute us.
Even our closest friends might leave when we need them the most.
But Jesus will always be with us.
It is better for our friends that we not follow them but follow Jesus.
In the end we all will receive the benefit of following Jesus.

We love You, beautiful Jesus.

55

Good News, Bad News

What determines whether news is good or bad?

What appears to be good news to us may displease God.
What appears to be bad news to us may
please Him and be good news to Him.

What is it about bad news that we hate so much?
It seems that generating good news and running
from bad news is what drives us.

We call anything that saves us from pain good news,
and whatever brings us trouble we call bad news.
Jesus' life speaks the exact opposite of this mentality.
The true good news of Jesus brings pain and persecution
but also the greatest joy known to man.

Most of the world is running away from the good news of the gospel.
Even when God Almighty appeared on earth,
in the Old Testament and the New Testament,
people ran away and rejected Him.
He is not always welcomed as the Holy Spirit even in our time.

When Jesus was arrested and then crucified,
it was bad news to all who loved Him.
But what many people called bad news ended up being the best news ever,
the news that saves all mankind.

Holy Spirit, help us to see the truth behind
what we call good news and bad news.
Help us not to be affected by news anymore.
We want to be affected by You.

56

Feelings or Healing?

One night I asked the Holy Spirit to fill my heart,
and I felt Him as I had many times before.
Later on that night I got so angry at my wife for no reason.
A lot of anger was coming out of my heart
that I didn't even know was there.

I asked the Holy Spirit, "Is this the fruit of being filled by You?"
This is what I saw in my heart:
When God enters a place there will be shaking and sometimes offense.
Yes, there will be healing also, but you never
know how the healing will come.

And they came to Jerusalem.
And He entered the temple and began to cast out
those who were buying and selling in the temple,
and overturned the tables of the money changers
and the seats of those who were selling doves;
and He would not permit anyone to carry goods through the temple.

And He began to teach and say to them,
"Is it not written, My house shall be called a house of prayer for all the nations?
But you have made it a robbers' den."

And the chief priests and the scribes heard this,
and began seeking how to destroy Him;
for they were afraid of Him, for all the multitude was astonished at His teaching

(MARK 11:15-18).

He shook my heart that night and anger started
to come out that I didn't know I had.
When we ask the Holy Spirit to rush into our lives,
we need to know that everything will not always be pretty and clean.

We will be offended, and others will be offended.
What happened that night offended my wife
but later on she saw her part in it also.
The Lord did a mighty work in both of our
hearts and the end result was so beautiful.

Jesus offended many people and even shocked His own disciples.
The Holy Spirit is concerned about our healing more than our feelings.
When we invite the Holy Spirit into our lives,
our feelings might get hurt but our healing will be guaranteed.
His ways are different than our ways.
He knows how to deal with us and even makes us angry enough
to be honest with each other and with Him.
Isn't He wonderful?

57

His Ways Are Higher Than Right Ways

Dear Holy Spirit,
You told me to give You complete control of my heart every day.
May I get into the habit of asking You to show me Your ways every day
and acknowledge that Your ways are higher than my ways.

You deal with everything in such a unique way.
You sent Your own Son to rescue us through His death.
No one but You could ever come up with a plan like that.

The "right" way is as high as I can go.
But Your ways are higher than the right ways.
They are so different from what we call the "right" things or the "right" ways.

But I am human and I forget to ask You to show me Your ways.
As long as I do the right thing, I don't see
the need to ask You for Your ways.
That is when I get into trouble.

Now I choose Your ways over my ways and even over what I call the right ways.
I want Your ways.
My heart is crying out for Your ways.
Show my heart Your ways and not just the right ways.

"For My thoughts are not your thoughts,
Neither are your ways My ways," declares the LORD.

"For as the heavens are higher than the earth,
So are My ways higher than your ways
And My thoughts than your thoughts"

(ISAIAH 55:8-9).

I need You, Holy Spirit.
Please make me become addicted to You like I am addicted to Jesus Christ.

58

Releasing God into the World

People who don't have the Holy Spirit in their hearts are experiencing agony.
But I am realizing that people who have the Holy Spirit in their hearts
but don't know how to release Him out into
the world are experiencing agony also.

I feel so uncomfortable sometimes,
and my agony and discomfort lead me to try
to do more or to be a better person.
But it is not about being a better person,
it is about allowing the better One to come out of us.

I never had peace until God came into my heart.
Now I don't have peace until I release Him out of my heart into the world.

Holy Spirit, show me how to release You.
I am burning inside with Your fire.
You don't want to stay inside; You want to go out.
Release me from my agony by being released out of me.
You are burning to get out.

But if I say, "I will not remember Him
Or speak anymore in His name,"
Then in my heart it becomes like a burning fire
Shut up in my bones;
And I am weary of holding it in,
And I cannot endure it

(JEREMIAH 20:9).

Who brought God into my heart?
Christ through His Holy Spirit.

Who can release God out of my heart into the world?
Christ through His Holy Spirit.
Until then, I will be in agony.

The Holy Spirit brought Christ into my heart when I was a Shiite Muslim.
Now as a Christian the Holy Spirit will release Christ
out of me into the world.

We need You, Holy Spirit.
Help us to express You from our hearts in a unique way out into the world.
In Your beautiful name, Amen.

59

No More Hiding

God the Father, the Son, and the Holy Spirit all have a part to play
in our salvation and our walk with God.
In a simple way we can say they all have to do their part.

God the Father finished His part by sending His Son, Jesus, to us.
God the Son finished His part by shedding
His own blood on the cross for us.
God the Holy Spirit started His part 2,000 years ago in a very unique way.
He appeared on earth after Jesus ascended into heaven.
Now let us see how people responded to the
Godhead when they appeared on earth.

When God the Father appeared to the Israelites,
they were afraid and ran away when they heard His voice.
They hid behind Moses and told him to talk to God on their behalf.
Somehow God the Father seemed scary,
and the people were afraid and even offended by His voice and actions.

**And all the people perceived the thunder and the lightning flashes
and the sound of the trumpet and the mountain smoking;
and when the people saw it, they trembled and stood at a distance.**

**Then they said to Moses,
"Speak to us yourself and we will listen;
but let not God speak to us, lest we die"**

(EXODUS 20:18-19).

When God the Son appeared, the Pharisees were
offended and afraid of Him also.
They hid behind God the Father and didn't want
anything to do with God the Son.
They were doing what God the Father told them to do regarding the law.

It was not just the Pharisees whom the Son of God offended.
Even common people who saw His miracles
were offended and left Him when He said:

"He who eats My flesh and drinks My blood abides in Me, and I in him"

(JOHN 6:56).

Then after Jesus left the earth, God the Holy Spirit appeared on earth.
So many people still to this day are offended by the
Holy Spirit and hide behind Christ. They say:
"We have Jesus Christ and don't want anything to do with the Holy Spirit.
We read our Bibles and do what the Bible tells us to do."

It appears to me that God will always look offensive when He appears
and His presence will cause many to manifest,
run away, and find places to hide.

See, God the Father didn't look offensive to the Pharisees
because they didn't live in the time when He appeared to Moses.
We as Christians are not offended by Jesus
because we are not living in the time when He walked on earth.

I can't imagine what Peter felt when Jesus told him,

"Get behind Me, Satan"

(SEE MARK 8:33).

I would be offended, wouldn't you?

We are not in the time that God the Father and God the Son
manifested themselves on earth.
We are in the time that God the Holy Spirit
is manifesting Himself on earth.
Are we running from the Holy Spirit like those
people ran from the Father and the Son?
As we know from the Bible, few people got past their feelings and offenses
to stay around the Father and Son when they were manifested on earth.
Can we bypass our offenses and stay with the Holy Spirit?

No matter how offensive He seems, there is no place to run or hide anymore.

Beautiful and magnificent Holy Spirit,
forgive us for hiding behind Christ as an excuse for not following You.
Forgive us for hiding behind our own agendas, wisdom,
and works as an excuse to reject You.
We want You and we need You.
We will give You full permission to do anything You want with our lives.
No more running and hiding behind the Godhead.
You are so beautiful, my love.

60

Run Toward His Voice

There are many voices everywhere around us—
voices that come from every direction, out of the people around us,
our friends and family members, TV, news, books and tapes,
the wisdom of man,
the voice of reason, shame, temptation, guilt, etc.
Which voice should we listen to?

Sometimes the voices around us get so loud that we can't hear
the voice of our Lord anymore.
I believe one of the reasons that the Lord spoke to
the Israelites with a loud voice
was to cancel out all the other voices in their heads.
Of course His loud voice could also help protect
them from temptation, sin, and doubt.

They didn't know God personally.
They didn't know how precious, beautiful, and selfless He is.
They thought God came to show off and to kill them.

Now that we have Christ in us and know how beautiful He is,
we should search for and run toward His voice
and allow His voice to cancel out all others.
We must practice hearing Him and ignoring the others.

Holy Spirit, be so loud in our lives!
Help us to follow Your voice.
We want to be so in love with the sound of Your voice inside of us.

61

Deep Worship

I once asked the Lord to speak to me about worship.
He said to my heart,
"When you come to Me and don't focus on anything but Me,
that is the deepest form of worship.
Come to Me and don't remember your job, your spouse,
or even your Christianity;
just remember Me."

It made sense to me because in marriage when people are intimate,
they don't have their normal, everyday clothes on—
they get naked.
In deep worship we can also strip ourselves of our thoughts
and any attachments and go to the Lord naked.

I hope you can hear my heart in this.
All I am saying is that we need to get intimate with the Lord in our hearts
and go to Him without any attachments sometimes—
with empty, naked minds.
In marriage we don't walk around naked all the time,
but there is a time to be intimate.

I hope I didn't make you uncomfortable.
Adam and Eve were naked in front of the Lord.
Of course with us it is not a physical thing, it takes place in our hearts.
We go to Him empty of everything and meet with Him.
This is one way of touching His heart.
Are you ready?

62

Christ Over Christianity

Is it possible that Christianity could take the place of Christ Himself?
When we face sin or temptation,
we have a tendency to remind ourselves that we are Christians,
and Christians don't do this or that.
When you face temptation, don't remember
that you are a Christian, remember Christ.
Let us remind ourselves of Christ Jesus and allow
Him to help us do the right thing.

The right thing cannot lead us to the right One,
but the right One can lead us to the right thing.
Our focus is not on Christianity, but on Christ Himself.

It is very hard to stop thinking about being Christians.
Our minds have been carrying this thought for so long.
It is very deep in our subconscious.
May the Lord help us to replace Christianity with Christ.

In most cases we think about Christianity more than Christ.
When we face temptation or sin we remind ourselves of the fact that we are
Christians, and as Christians we can't do this.
We remind ourselves of a bunch of dos and don'ts.
What happened to the sweet Jesus we met as baby Christians
when we first gave our hearts to Him?
What happened to our Jesus?
Has He been replaced by Christianity?

Christianity should not overshadow Christ.
Christ should overshadow Christianity

When you see sin, remember Christ.
When you face temptation, remember Christ.

When you see problems, remember Christ.
When you face pain and suffering, remember Christ.
When you are hopeless and discouraged, remember Christ.
In all things remember Christ.
There are many other things we remember every day.
Sometimes it feels like torture to remember all the problems and obstacles.
Remember Jesus instead of all the things that are hurting you.
Remember Him.
He is the Beginning and the End.
He is all revelations combined together.

May the Lord forgive us for putting Christianity over Christ.
Come back to us, sweet Jesus.
Allow us to remember You.

63

Professional Hunters of Success and Blessings

The hunt for success and blessings is taking most of our attention and time,
causing us to lose our closeness to the One who taught us how to hunt.

Some of us are so professional in our hunting.
Some of us are not very good hunters but we want to be.
Some of us read books and study to become better hunters of blessings and success.

Why are we so eager to be successful and blessed?

It is good to be blessed and successful in our Christian walks,
but if we make our lives and the blessings we receive about ourselves,
we will grow away from the One whom the blessings and success come from.
Sometimes when we run after our prey as hunters of success,
we become prey for the enemy.

Some say that we should claim our blessings and
enter into our promised land.
I say yes and amen to that!
But when we enter into our promised land, who and what will we live for,
the blessings and success or the One who brought them?
I leave the answer to our hearts.

May we claim our blessings for the purpose of growing closer to Christ
and expanding His kingdom and for no other reason.

It is a very dangerous business to live for self.
We will become easy prey for the enemy when we live for self.
We have perfect protection when we live for Christ.
Let us hide in Him and live for Him.
He will share all He has with us.
He will not keep it all for Himself.
He is love and love does not seek it's own.

64

Insurance on Earth and in Heaven

Our lives in heaven are insured by the blood of Jesus.
Let us insure our lives on earth.

How do we do this?
By living for Christ, not self.

Which insurance agent should we go to?
The Holy Spirit.

**For not one of us lives for himself, and not one dies for himself;
for if we live, we live for the Lord, or if we die, we die for the Lord;
therefore whether we live or die, we are the Lord's.**

(ROMANS 14:7-8)

To live for Christ is to purchase the best insurance of all time.
When we live for Christ with the help of the Holy Spirit,
we get perfect coverage on earth.

There is no insurance when we live for self.
That is why there is so much pain when we live for self.
It doesn't matter how wealthy and successful we become,
it is very dangerous and painful to live for self.
Let us center every aspect of our lives around Christ Jesus.

Now, let us talk about the coverage and benefits.
We will be insured to carry the love of God in us.
We will be free from self, which is a huge blessing.
We will be mostly covered from the arrows of rejection,
fear of man, jealousy, anger, judgment, and all other arrows
that come from the enemy.
We will carry so much peace and contentment.

Therefore I am well content with weaknesses, with insults, with distresses,
with persecutions, with difficulties, for Christ's sake;
for when I am weak, then I am strong.

(II CORINTHIANS 12:10)

Living for Christ is very good insurance with the best benefits and coverage.

What is the price?
Jesus paid a price with His blood, and we have a price to pay as well.
If the Lord paid the price, why do we need to pay a price?
Let us see the price that the Lord requires us to pay.

I told the Lord once,
"Lord, You saved me from hell, now save me from myself."

Self is the price He wants us to pay.
He wants to free us from ourselves.
To live for self is to experience hell on earth.
We are all saved through His blood from eternal hell,
but there is a hell on earth for those who don't
purchase insurance from Jesus.
Of course, this is what I personally believe;
you should be honest with your own heart and with God.
Yes my friend, when we give up self and make everything about Jesus,
we have the perfect insurance coverage on earth.

Don't walk on earth without insurance, my friend.
The Holy Spirit wants to sign us in.
Are you in?

65

The Name of Jesus

Sometimes we get to the point that we can't even find any words to pray.
Sometimes depression and hopelessness are all that is left.

I remember having a very bad migraine headache one night.
I tried so hard to pray it off of me and it didn't work.
I tried to confess any possible sins.
It didn't work.
I tried to remember any revelation the Lord had given
me to stop the migraine.
It didn't work.
I was so desperate.
*Suddenly the idea came to me to say the name of Jesus
over and over again and I did.*
After a few moments the headache left me.

The Lord spoke to my heart and reminded me of
something He had told me before.
He said, "Because Jesus is the Beginning and the End,
when you say the name of Jesus you say all that needs to be said."

When you have nothing to say, just say the name of Jesus.
That is all that needs to be said.

Let us cling to His beautiful and powerful name.

66

Loving All People and All Things

After I gave my heart to the Lord, He started to
teach me about unconditional love,
which is to love people no matter what they do or don't do, even our enemies.

The Lord is teaching me to love all things.
First, He started to teach me the importance of loving all people.
Now He is teaching me the importance of loving all things,
including hardship and tests.

And we know that God causes all things
to work together for good to those who love God,
to those who are called according to His purpose (Romans 8:28).

Love is patient, love is kind, and is not jealous;
love does not brag and is not arrogant,

does not act unbecomingly;
it does not seek its own, is not provoked,
does not take into account a wrong suffered,

does not rejoice in unrighteousness, but rejoices with the truth;

bears all things, believes all things, hopes all things, endures all things.

(I CORINTHIANS 13:4-7)

Joseph was betrayed by his own brothers, which led to slavery and
imprisonment.
He could have been afraid of his situation.
He could have hated his brothers for it.
He had a choice to hate his situation or to embrace it and trust his Creator.

We know that the Lord will allow many difficult situations

to come to pass in our lives like He allowed for Job,
Joseph, Elijah, Moses, David, and many others.

The Lord didn't even exclude His own Son.
When His Son faced what was in front of Him,
in one difficult moment He asked for the cup to be removed.
But in the next sentence He said, "Your will, not mine, Father"
(see Matthew 26:39).
He embraced the Father's love though it came
in an act of pain, betrayal, and death.

Jesus didn't hate what He faced, so why should we?
If we don't embrace hardship, it will lead to fear and hate.

The Lord wants to set us free from fear and hate.
Let us not fear the situations we are in.
Let us not hate the difficulties anymore.
Let us learn to love even the hardships.

When we start learning to love all things, fear and hate will leave us alone.
Some of us are afraid of many situations that we are in.
How many times have we said:
"I hate the fact that…" or "I hate that I have to face…" or "I am afraid of…"?

May the Lord free us from fear and hatred.
Love will give us freedom.
Can you imagine being able to love all people and all things?
Maybe we can call it unconditional submission without fear and hate.
To me, that is the definition of freedom.
Let us be free, free to love all people, free to even love all things.
The Lord wants to see us free to love.

67

Hell on Earth

Christians will not experience hell after life
because the blood of Christ already saved us from that.
But is it possible as a Christian to experience hell on earth?
Yes, I believe so.

For a period of two weeks I felt so uncomfortable in my soul
and could not find the reason.
I got to the place that I could not take it anymore.
I called my brother and told him about it.
He asked me to explain how I felt.
I told him I felt fear around me for no reason.
I felt like something was wrong but I did not know what.
I felt something bad was going to happen, but I didn't know when.

I asked him if he could come to our house and pray for me.
I couldn't shake what I was feeling,
and in that moment I knew why some people commit suicide.
I was experiencing hell on earth.

Let us talk about hell for a moment.
How was hell built?
What kind of material was used to build hell?
I believe Satan is responsible for the existence of hell
and that the material used to build it was LIES.
Lies are all he has.
As Christians we are completely saved from hell after death
but not necessarily during life on earth.

Satan is capable of building hell on earth using the same material.
He builds hell around us, one lie at a time.
Every time we believe one of his lies he adds another brick,
and the walls of hell become higher and higher around us.

After spending some time with the Lord,
He showed me why I was having such a hard time in those two weeks.
I had believed some lies about myself and some situations I was in.
By allowing those lies to get into my heart,
the enemy created hell around me.
After recognizing this truth,
I searched my heart to find those lies
and the Holy Spirit helped me to recognize and renounce them.
Soon the feeling of being in hell left me.

There are many people around us who are living in hell
every single day even as Christians.
Imagine the hell that the unsaved are living in.
Let us build heaven around others and ourselves
with the light of the truth that comes from God.
If you are experiencing hell, know that some lies
have gotten into your heart.
Ask the Holy Spirit to shine His truth into your
life and the situations you are in.
Remember, Satan uses lies to create hell around us.

"Whenever he speaks a lie, he speaks from his own nature;
for he is a liar, and the father of lies" (see John 8:44).

Truth comes out of God and lies come out of Satan.
Let us see what the Lord says about us.
Satan has many things to say about others and us.
Since he is the father of lies, let us not listen to him but to the Lord.
Let us ask the Holy Spirit to tear down the walls of hell in our lives
and let us experience heaven on earth. May the Word of God be our shield and
protect us from hell.

"'For I know the plans that I have for you,' declares the LORD,
'plans for welfare and not for calamity to give you a future and a hope.

'Then you will call upon Me and come and pray to Me, and I will listen to you.

'And you will seek Me and find Me when you search
for Me with all your heart'".

(JEREMIAH 29:11-13)

We need to know the truth about ourselves and others.
We should face the truth every single day and we should spread the truth.
The lost that are living in buildings of hell will be drawn to temples of truth.

Truth will tear down the strongholds of Satan.
When we give encouraging words to someone,
we are telling the truth about them from God's prospective,
and that will set them free.

Prayer:
I renounce any lies that I carry.
Holy Spirit, go deep into my soul and expose those
lies and replace them with truth.
In Jesus' name.

Tell me what *You* think of me, God.
I want to know the truth.

People want to know what God thinks of them.
Don't you, my friend?

68

Messengers of Love or Messengers of Condemnation

*"And do not judge and you will not be judged;
and do not condemn, and you will not be condemned;
pardon, and you will be pardoned".*

(LUKE 6:37)

*The faith which you have, have as your own conviction before God.
Happy is he who does not condemn himself in what he approves.*

(ROMANS 14:22)

*Therefore you are without excuse, every man of you who passes judgment,
for in that you judge another, you condemn yourself;
for you who judge practice the same things.*

(ROMANS 2:1)

How beautiful life will be when we stop condemning others and ourselves.
Even God paid a very high price to not condemn us, the work of His hands.
Death is condemnation and condemnation is death.
Christ came to destroy condemnation once and for all from our lives.

Please don't condemn others.
If you do, you are greatly damaging them.
How many times a day do we condemn ourselves and our work?
How many times a day do we condemn people and what they do?

*We should not allow the powers of darkness to use
us as messengers of condemnation.
We should be used by the Holy Spirit to be the messengers of the grace and love of
God.*

Release anyone whom you have ever condemned in your heart.
Release them now in Christ's name.
Set them free.
Call their names in your heart and release them
from the power of your condemnation.
Call their names in your heart and bless them.
Read Jeremiah 29:11 over them in your heart.

Don't allow Satan to make you his messenger.
Be God's messengers of grace and love.
Can you hear the call?
God is calling for messengers.
Do you want to become one?
We are messengers of grace, messengers of love,
messengers of the gospel, messengers of salvation,
messengers of the kingdom.

69

In Myself and in Him

The realization that we are sinners will allow us to touch the throne of grace.

**It is a trustworthy statement, deserving full acceptance,
that Christ Jesus came into the world to save sinners,
among whom I am foremost of all.**

(I TIMOTHY 1:15)

According to Apple Dictionary, the word "foremost" means:
"the most prominent in rank, importance, or position."

Paul knew who he was in himself.
He also knew who he was in Christ.
May the Lord open our eyes daily to see who we are in Him
and who we are in ourselves.
*We are the foremost of sinners in ourselves,
but in Christ we are without any blame.*

Give me this daily realization, Jesus.
When I see who I am in me,
it will keep me from becoming proud of my good works like the Pharisees,
and when I see who I am in You,
it will help me to love You more than anything else.

**"For this reason I say to you, her sins, which are many,
have been forgiven, for she loved much;
but he who is forgiven little, loves little".**

(LUKE 7:47)

This daily realization will lead us into His daily grace,
and grace is what we need.
In this place, the Scripture above will apply to us as it did to Mary.

How are we going to be forgiven much and love much
if we don't see who we are in ourselves?

Of course we will not stop with this revelation.
We will move up and touch the throne of His grace.
One of the reasons that new converts to Christianity love Jesus so much
is that they know how much He has forgiven them.
They have no problem realizing their sins.

Let's do our homework every day.
We must meditate on who we are in ourselves and who we are in Him.
This will keep our love fresh for Christ.

70

God Doesn't Want to Be Rescued

Are we trying to rescue God sometimes?
Are we trying to rescue God's movement?
We can't rescue God.
God doesn't need anyone to rescue Him.
Jesus didn't want to be rescued by Peter in the following passage:

From that time Jesus began to show His disciples that He must go to Jerusalem,
and suffer many things from the elders and chief priests and scribes,
and be killed, and be raised up on the third day.

And Peter took Him aside and began to rebuke Him, saying,
"God forbid it, Lord! This shall never happen to You."

But He turned and said to Peter, "Get behind Me, Satan!
You are a stumbling block to Me;
for you are not setting your mind on God's interests, but man's"

(MATTHEW 16:21-23).

We can't rescue revival or God's movement.
Let us relax and give all things into the hands of the Lord.
He doesn't need to be rescued.
He is so much mightier than that.
He wants to be loved, obeyed, and ushered in.
He knows what He wants and He is going to
do what He said He would do.
The angels were not allowed to rescue Him on the cross,
so why should we try to do so?
It may appear at times that God needs our help.
It may appear that God is still on the cross.
It may appear that He is suffering and needs our assistance.

Out of the goodness of our hearts we try to rescue Him and His movement,
but He doesn't need or want to be rescued.
He gets offended when we try to rescue Him.

Imagine if the angels had rescued Christ from the cross.
There would be no resurrection power in Christ.

But when they came to the threshing floor of Nacon,
Uzzah reached out toward the ark of God and took hold of it,
for the oxen nearly upset it.

And the anger of the LORD burned against Uzzah,
and God struck him down there for his irreverence;
and he died there by the ark of God.

(II SAMUEL 6:6-7)

God can take care of Himself and His movement.
The Bible says obedience is better than sacrifice (see I Samuel 15:22).
We can also say that obedience is better than a rescue mission.
Our mission is to love, obey, and serve.
We are not on a rescue mission.

71

From Revelation to Visitation

Sometimes we receive revelations from the Lord
when we read the Bible or listen to a sermon.
This is how it works in my case:
The Holy Spirit will highlight some truth and allow
me to see it in a deeper way.
I call that a revelation from the Lord.

The Bible is full of revelations, and as we spend time with the Lord,
He opens our eyes to some of them.

What should we do with those revelations?
I believe those revelations should be made into visitations.
Those revelations should visit our hearts and also the hearts of others.
But it should start in our hearts first.

What good is a revelation if it doesn't enter into our hearts,
but stays in our brains instead?
When we allow a revelation to visit our hearts,
then it can go out of our hearts and visit other people.

It is easy to go to seminars and receive revelations,
however, it may not be as easy to turn them into visitations.
But how long should we wait?
Time is quickly passing by.
Let us move on and stop circling the same mountain over and over again.
As soon as you get a revelation or a highlighted truth,
ask the Holy Spirit to take it into your heart.
Let us ask the One who gave us revelations to
make them into visitations.

From His dwelling place He looks out
On all the inhabitants of the earth,

He who fashions the hearts of them all,
He who understands all their works

(PSALM 33:14-15).

If He gave you the revelation, then He will help you to make it into a visitation.

Cultivate our hearts with Your visitation, our Lord.
Fashion our hearts with Your visitation.

The Intentions of Our Hearts

Love is patient, love is kind, and is not jealous;
love does not brag and is not arrogant,
does not act unbecomingly;
it does not seek its own...

(I CORINTHIANS 13:4-5)

You ask and do not receive, because you ask with wrong motives,
so that you may spend it on your pleasures.

(JAMES 4:3)

"Therefore repent of this wickedness of yours, and pray the Lord that if possible, the
intention of your heart may be forgiven you."

(ACTS 8:22)

May the Lord help us to pay more attention to the intentions of our hearts
when we do things or when we ask Him for things.

Godly intentions will attract godly blessings.
Let us learn this lesson.
We will be surprised how many of God's blessings we will attract
when we make the intentions of our hearts right before God.
Even when you ask someone to help you out,
search for and find a good intention for your request.
See how your request will bring good fruit to their life
and to the kingdom of God.
Learn godly principles.
God doesn't seek His own and He wants His children to be like Him.
May we walk with godly intentions in our hearts before Him.
In His beautiful name.

73

Give Me Jesus

When the Holy Spirit gives you a revelation,
thank Him, but don't be satisfied by it.
Say to Him, "*Now give me Jesus.*"
When He gives you the desire of your heart, thank Him and say to Him,
"Now give me Jesus."

Sometimes I am so polite that I forget to love.
Sometimes I am so quick to search for the answer
and to give an answer that I forget to love.
I used to say to the Lord:
"Give me the answer; give me wisdom; give me revelation."
Now I say: "Give me Jesus."

I am dying, give me Jesus.
O give me Jesus and put me in the quest for love.

Graduation from the School of Love

We are all in the school of love.
We are all working to be good students and pass our tests every day.
I believe the only way to graduate from the school of love is to realize
we can't pass the tests in our own strength.
In our graduation ceremony our teacher and master will die for us
in order to graduate us.

It will even get worse. *We* have to do it.
We have to see our parts in His death 2,000 years ago.
We have to kill Him.
Otherwise we cannot graduate.

Some may say that He already died and we have
already accepted His blood,
therefore, we don't have to kill Him again.

I personally believe that we have to get the
revelation that we nailed Him on the cross.
It was KAMRAN who put the nails in His
hands and hammered them in.
It was KAMRAN who whipped Him, it was KAMRAN who killed Him.
It was me and it was you.

Most of us believe that the Pharisees caused His death,
and the Roman soldiers nailed Him to the cross.
My friend, it was you and I who did it.
He died for our sins, not just the sins of the Pharisees.
My sins nailed Him to the cross.

I used to believe that other people killed Jesus 2,000 years ago
and I received the benefit of His blood and got saved.
Now I believe that I killed Christ, and I am benefiting from His death.

This is true love—
not that we loved Him but that He loved us first
and allowed us to kill Him in order to save us.
Yes, our Master was killed by us, His students in the school of love.

Jesus, for once allow me to see myself nailing You to that cross.
I know what You did for me, now allow me to see what I did to You.
Allow me to graduate, my love.
You died for me and I killed You.
Now I can love You even more.
You always loved me, my love, Jesus.

75

Make a Love Story for Heaven to Watch

Only love will satisfy.
Only love will glorify.
Only love will bring us peace.
Only love will give us the courage we need.
Love is what I seek and desire.
I love love.

We are all desperate for love, and will remain
desperate until we learn to love.
Seek love, not the answer.
We always seek answers so that we may solve the problems we are facing.
We are desperate for the answer and when we find it,
it will not satisfy us until we find love and learn to love.
Start to spend more of your time making a love story.
There are many things to do; there are many demands.
The demands will never stop.
Spend your time making a love story.

When you set your heart and mind to make a love story,
you will feel so much of God's strength in you.
I love a good love story, how about you my friend?

Hollywood is making all kinds of movies.
Let us make love stories that will be shown in heaven forever.
We are movie makers; this is what we do.
All the events are real.
There are no actors or actresses.
The Lord is giving us a platform to perform and to make movies.
We are all in it together.
Let's make it fun.
Some of us are famous in heaven for our movies
and the stories of our daily lives.

Do you want to be famous on earth or in heaven?

Ask the Lord to help you make one of the best movies of the day.
Real joy and happiness will rush into your life when you make a love story
with the help of our lovely God.
It doesn't take a great amount of resources and money to make a love story.
One smile can make a love story,
or even warm hug, a word of encouragement, a simple prayer,
or just telling someone it is going to be okay.

How can I make a love story today, my Lord?
Allow us to tap into the joy of making a love story.
Allow me to read the Bible as a love story.
I want a love story today.

Great Distance in Our Hearts

You can love someone and at the same time be very far away from them in
your heart.
Expectation can come between loved ones and separate them so quietly.
To love without expectation is to enjoy your love.
Expectation can take away the joy of your love.
Expectation can cause a great distance between your heart and others.
You can love someone and still be so far away from them.
This can happen in marriages and all other relationships.

Check the distance of your heart from the Lord, your spouse, family,
friends, and even the people of the world.
Do to them what you expect from them.
Lay your expectation down for the sake of love.
Give all your expectation to Jesus.
Talk to Him about what you expect from others
and wait and see how He will take care of them.
It is very sad to walk around with a heart that is so far from people
because of our expectations.
Help us, Jesus, and bring our hearts close to one another.

The Ecstasy of Love and Romance

The world is so bored and wants to be entertained.
The world is after ecstasy.

What will get us out of our boredom?
What will give us ecstasy?

Passionate and true love will get the boredom
out of our lives and will bring ecstasy.
When the Lord told us to love, He didn't want to put a heavy burden on us.
He wanted to give us the honor of enjoying passionate love in our hearts.
To love God and others is an honor.

Are you bored?
Fight for passionate love in your heart toward God
and toward others and you will get free of boredom.
The richest person is the one who carries passionate love in his or her heart.

What are we waiting for?
Let us get out of boredom.
The Lord offers us the opportunity to live with the ecstasy of love.
May we live with the ecstasy of love in our hearts every single day.

Ecstasy is defined as
"an overwhelming feeling of great happiness or joyful excitement"
(Apple Dictionary).
Some get drunk by drinking alcohol because they are so bored.
Let us get drunk by accessing the love that God put in our hearts.

Our hearts can be a wine bottle that we can
drink from and share with others,
the wine of our passion and love for God and for others.

Let us drink the wine of love every single day and offer it to the world.
The world is thirsty.
The world is in desperate need of God's love.
The world is drunk with the wrong drink.
Let us give them the true wine of love.
Are you ready to get drunk and make the world drunk with romance,
passion, and the love of God?
The world is after ecstasy; let us offer them
the true ecstasy of the love of God.

Satan will pervert everything that is good.
We can get the original wine from the Lord.
Let us tap into it.
May the Lord be with us all.

**Babylon has been a golden cup in the hand of the LORD,
Intoxicating all the earth.
The nations have drunk of her wine;
Therefore the nations are going mad.**

**Suddenly Babylon has fallen and been broken;
Wail over her!
Bring balm for her pain;
Perhaps she may be healed.**

(JEREMIAH 51:7-8)

Why should we get drunk on something that destroys us?
God offered us the best quality drink of all ages:
love, passion, and romance.

Even the Lord desires our love, passion, and romance.
The Lord told me in my dream one night:
"Tell Me something romantic."

May we be romantic toward You, the Creator of romance.
May we fall in love with You, Jesus, every day throughout eternity.
Falling in love with You and staying in love is what we want.

*Why should we live a day without the ecstasy of love and romance
that comes from our wonderful God?*

The Truth Will Prove Itself

Most of our energy is spent on proving ourselves to each other.
It is a very hard and draining process.
Even in our teachings we try to prove our points.
I believe *the truth will prove itself.*
We don't have to prove anything.
All we need to do is teach and speak the truth in love.
Christ can prove His existence to people,
all we need to do is to speak the truth about Him
and leave the proving part to the Holy Spirit.
Remember, trying to prove the truth about
Christ is doing the Holy Spirit's job.

Our mission is not to prove anything to anyone;
our mission is to love and to speak the truth in love.
There will be no time left to love
if we spend all of our time and energy on proving the truth.
Truth will prove itself in the right time if it is revealed through love.

I am tired of proving myself to others.
I am tired of looking for the approval of man.
I am weary of trying so hard to prove the truth.
Help me, Jesus.

Evangelism should not involve trying to prove anything.
The Holy Spirit will prove anything that needs to be proven.
We will rest in the Holy Spirit when we stop trying to prove our points.

Treat Each Day as a Lifetime

What is your view of just a single day of your life?
I believe we should look at a single day the same way we look at a lifetime.
I believe the way we view a single day should change a little.

Why do our views need to change?
Because Satan wants to steal our lives one day at a time.
When we don't give value to one day and even, to a degree, disrespect one day,
he will easily steal that day from us.

Satan will use all of his tools like depression, anxiety,
hopelessness, anger, greed, selfishness, etc.,
to waste just one day of our lives.
One day is very important.
That one day *is* your life.
Guard each day as you guard your life.

What should we do to stop Satan from stealing our days?
Learn to respect one day as you respect your life.

Yes, you will have many days in your life.
You have 365 days in one year,
but the truth is, Satan wants to steal your life one day at a time.
When you lose one day to evil, you have lost your life on that day.

See one day as you see your lifetime.
When you respect one day,
you start to become younger and younger at heart,
and the joy of the Lord will be all over you.

**This is the day which the LORD has made;
Let us rejoice and be glad in it.**

(PSALM 118:24)

> And there are also many other things which Jesus did,
> which if they were written in detail,
> I suppose that even the world itself would not contain the books
> which were written.

(JOHN 21:25)

Remember, Jesus accomplished all those things in three years.
Sometimes we think there is always tomorrow,
and that keeps us from tapping into God's plan and purpose for today.
Yes, we all have lifetime callings, but how about the call of each day?

There are many things we wait to do until tomorrow.
Even resting can be something we plan to do in the future.

These are some of the things we put off for tomorrow:
praying, reading the Bible,
spending quality time with God and tapping into His rest,
spending quality time with friends and family,
being romantically involved with Jesus and getting to know Him more,
healing the sick, casting out demons, preaching the good news,
helping others get to know Jesus,
being filled with and spreading God's love,
helping the poor, the needy, the widows, and the orphans,
going after the desires of our hearts,
and accomplishing what God gave us to accomplish.

Satan wants to promote the idea that there is always tomorrow,
and through that he will steal our callings one day at a time.
*If we would treat a each day as a lifetime,
we could tap into eternity on earth.*

> ...who has saved us and called us with a holy calling,
> not according to our works,
> but according to His own purpose and grace
> which was granted us in Christ Jesus from all eternity.

(II TIMOTHY 1:9)

One day is so precious; we should guard it as we guard our lives.
We should not spend time in our day in anger,
selfishness, hopelessness, anxiety,
lack of faith, guilt, shame, disbelief, worries, or any other evil.
Satan will use all of these things to steal and waste our time.
When you face any evil that is wasting your life, say to it,
"I have no time for you in my day anymore.
You have wasted my life one day at a time.
No more will I allow you to steal what God gave me.
I will guard my day with the help of the Holy Spirit.
I will tap into the call of the day and through
that I will tap into eternity on earth."

Yes, tapping into our callings is tapping into eternity,
and that is why Satan comes to steal our lives one day at a time.
If someone came to literally take our lives away,
would we allow them to take them away easily?
No, we would fight for our lives.
Then we should not allow the enemy to take our days away.

When you look at one day as you look at your life,
then you tap into eternity on earth.
Satan comes to steal your life one day at a time.
He comes to steal your lifetime calling one day at a time
by keeping you away from your call of the day.

Each day when you wake up, think of that day as the most
important day of your life. Watch out for any negative plans
that may try to sneak in and steal time from this day.

Help me, Lord, to treat one day as a lifetime.
Allow me to respect a single day and spend it as I spend my life.
Then I will have 365 lifetimes in one year,
and there is no telling what You will do through me.

80

A Famine of Love

What will happen if we see people dying all around us?
What will happen if we see lions tearing people apart as prey?
What will happen if we see people burning in fire in front of us?
Those things are happening every day in
many places and many ways around the world.

Are we ready to see it?
How strong are we?

Satan is strong. Satan is a lion.
He tears people apart.
He burns them with his lies and fear.
He comes to kill, steal, and destroy (see John 10:10).
He hates us.

People are dying of love hunger
There is a famine in the land, a famine of love.
There is plenty of hate, selfishness, fear, lies, depression, anxiety,
hopelessness, anger, and frustration.
There is an enormous lack of love.
There is a famine of love.

But we have access to the Lord of love.
So what is the problem then?
Where is love?
Are we interested in loving?
Is there hope for the world?
Yes.
God is love.
His Son is proof of that.

May the love of Jesus through us burn down the lies of Satan.

May there be a famine of lies and hate.
May the Lord teach us to love so the world will see His hope in us
and be saved from the famine of love.

81

Led by His Aroma

Different people use different kinds of perfume or cologne.
Usually we pick our favorites and stick to them.
But the Lord Jesus has unlimited fragrances for His people.
He has a certain aroma for those who know Him personally.
For each individual He has a different aroma,
and everyone has their own aroma of Jesus to follow.
In our personal walks with Jesus He will lead us every single day
through the particular aroma that we know of Him.
It is very important to be led by His aroma.

Sometimes we follow the crowd instead of following Jesus' aroma.
When Jesus walked on the earth the crowd followed Him around
because He fed them and healed them,
but the crowd left Him when He offended them through some of His
preaching.
Even His own disciples left Him.
But one of His disciples stood by Him to the very end,
the one who knew His aroma in a very personal way.

There was reclining on Jesus' breast one of His disciples, whom Jesus loved.

(JOHN 13:23)

There will be a time that the crowd will leave Jesus.
We can't follow the crowd.
We must follow Jesus' aroma for ourselves.
If we keep our heads close to His chest,
then we will know His aroma like Apostle John knew it
and we will follow Him to the very end,
even when the crowds are not there.

Now let us talk about Jesus' aroma that we are not familiar with.
The first step is to get to know the particular aroma

that He releases for us as individuals and to be led by it.
The second step is to go further ahead and get to know the different aromas
that He uses for different people.

Perhaps you go to a meeting and do not recognize the aroma of Jesus that you
are used to. That doesn't mean He is not there.
He might be releasing an aroma that you are not familiar with.

Ask Him to reveal His different aromas to you
so that you might know where He is in all people and all meetings.

We want to get to know Your aromas, Jesus, the Son of God, Most High.
In Your beautiful name.

82

The Factory of Good News

The enemy will magnify all of your problems.
He will tell you how large your problems are.
He will make a big deal out of all the small and unimportant
things you face every day.
He will even bring fear to you when you receive blessings.
He will try to make your life a factory of bad news.
What we see is not what is really there.
Let us ask the Lord to open our eyes to see what He sees.

The enemy will make a big deal out of
every small detail or obstacle you face
in order to make what the Lord told you to do a very small deal.
He will try to make all the big things that we are
supposed to pay attention to seem small,
and he will try to make all the small things seem big.

Make a big deal out of what the Lord says.
Focus on what the Lord told you to do.

One of the reasons we are so horrified is that
we allow Satan to make a big deal
out of even the smallest problems we face.

The big deal is Christ and His death and resurrection.
The big deal is to have the Holy Spirit inside of us.
The big deal is His will.
The big deal is to get to heaven through His blood.
HE is the big deal.

The enemy is like a factory of bad news.
He will make bad news out of everything.
Sometimes he is even capable of making

bad news using godly blessings.
The enemy made the good news of the gospel into bad news
for Muslims and many others.

Holy Spirit, we are ready to see and hear the
good news that is everywhere around us
and overlook the bad news.

Our Lord Jesus is the factory of good news and love.
May the Lord rebuke the factory of bad news out of our lives.
May the Lord rebuke you, Satan.

83

The Land of Love

Recently my brother faced a family crisis.
I wanted to help him out, to rescue him, and I couldn't.
Slowly shame and guilt started to get into me until it became unbearable.
I went before the Lord to ask Him to show me how I could help my brother.

But the Lord wanted to release me from the grip of shame and guilt.
He told me to love my brother in my
heart and meditate on my love for him.
That is all He wanted me to do, and when I started to meditate on my love for
my brother, the shame and guilt left my heart.

In that moment I realized that the only place
Satan cannot follow us is the land of love.
Satan can get us in the land of knowledge, fairness, and right and wrong.
He can even chase us in the land of goodness.
Satan can put his feet into any land you go into but the land of love.
Always walk in the land of love and you will be safer than you could imagine.

Are you walking in the land of goodness, kindness, or fairness
so that you will be safe from Satan?
Satan can follow you even there.
Allow the Lord to take you to the land of love and start your journey there,
then you can be kind, fair, and gentle.
When you walk in the land of love,
you don't have to be perfect in order to be safe.
Your safety comes from the land, not your actions.
May we all enter into the land of the love of our Father.
May we receive our safety from the love of our Father in heaven.
There is safety in that land.

84

Lost in God

Being lost is not a pleasant feeling at all.
Picture yourself lost in a city or while driving.
We normally desire to find our way out of being lost.
We want to know how to find the right way.

How about being lost in God?
Have you ever felt that you don't know where God is taking you next?
Have you ever felt that you are lost in God Himself?
You trusted in Him, but nothing about
Him and His ways is making sense to you.
Should we try to find our way out of being lost
in God by trying to figure Him out?
No.
Is it safe to be lost in God?
Yes.

What does it mean to be lost in God?
Total trust without any reasoning—not knowing and still trusting.
When we trust ourselves totally in God's hands
we are losing ourselves in Him.
To have faith is to lose yourself in God.
To me the safest place to be lost is in God.
No matter where we end up in God, we are safe.
When you get lost in a city you may end up in a bad neighborhood,
but there is no bad neighborhood in God.

We get lost in His mercy and grace.
We get lost in His kindness, gentleness, and Fatherhood.
Even when you don't see any of the above, it is still safe to be lost in God.
When we get comfortable by being lost in God,
then nothing will worry us anymore.
In that stage our fear will have no power over us.

When we lose ourselves in God, nothing will surprise us anymore.
In that stage we are so dependent on Him
that nothing is a shock to us anymore,
even our own failures.
Until we learn to lose ourselves in God,
we will suffer fear, anxiety, and weariness.

"Abide in Me, and I in you.
As the branch cannot bear fruit of itself unless it abides in the vine,
so neither can you, unless you abide in Me.

"I am the vine, you are the branches;
he who abides in Me, and I in him, he bears much fruit,
for apart from Me you can do nothing."

(JOHN 15:4-5)

He who dwells in the shelter of the Most High
Will abide in the shadow of the Almighty.

I will say to the LORD, "My refuge and my fortress,
My God, in whom I trust!"

For it is He who delivers you from the snare of the trapper,
And from the deadly pestilence.

He will cover you with His pinions,
And under His wings you may seek refuge;
His faithfulness is a shield and bulwark.

You will not be afraid of the terror by night,
Or of the arrow that flies by day;

Of the pestilence that stalks in darkness,
Or of the destruction that lays waste at noon.

A thousand may fall at your side,
And ten thousand at your right hand;
But it shall not approach you.

You will only look on with your eyes
And see the recompense of the wicked.

For you have made the LORD, my refuge,
Even the Most High, your dwelling place.

No evil will befall you,
Nor will any plague come near your tent

(PSALM 91:1-10).

May I be lost in God and rejoice over it.
I was lost in my sin, now I am lost in God.
We are all called to be lost, not in the world or in our sins, but in Jesus.
Let's call in the lost to get lost in God.

When we get lost in Jesus, we can find everything we need in Him.
Everything can be found in Christ.
The deeper we travel in Him, the more we find what we need.
The more we get lost in Jesus, the more we find what we are looking for.
There is nothing to fear when we are lost in Him.
What is going to happen to you?
What is the worst thing that could happen while you are lost in Him?
Don't be afraid of trying new things anymore.
You are lost in God.
Don't be afraid of making mistakes.
When you lose yourself in God,
it is His responsibility to take care of you
and even to take care of your mistakes.
Be bold and courageous to jump in and make mistakes.
Nothing bad will happen.
Get lost in God.

85

Who Was, Who Is, Who Is to Come

**And the four living creatures, each one of them having six wings,
are full of eyes around and within; and day and night they do not cease to say,
"Holy, Holy, Holy, is the Lord God, the Almighty,
who was and who is and who is to come"**

(REVELATION 4:8)

Many of us believe that our Lord *was*.
We believe He came to earth and He *was* so powerful.
We also believe one day He will return and in
His return He will again be so powerful.
But few of us believe that He *is* powerful now in our lives.

We believe that HE WAS AND IS TO COME, but not that HE IS.
When we get the revelation that HE IS, our lives will be so **different**.

When we think of God creating the whole earth in seven days,
we think of His ability to accomplish things.
When we think about how He appeared to the Israelites,
we think of His might and power.
When we think about how He came to earth as a man named **Jesus,**
we think of all the miracles, signs, and wonders.
Also when we think of the day Jesus will come riding on the **clouds,**
it is hard to describe or imagine.
How about now?
What do we think of Him now in the present?
Is our God as powerful as He was and will be when He **returns?**

HE IS AS POWERFUL NOW AS HE WAS OR WILL EVER **BE.**

Lord, give us the revelation of who You are now.
When Moses asked Your name You said,

"I AM WHO I AM"

(EXODUS 3:14)

I AM is now.
May we know you as I AM.
Now.

86

Jesus Is the Result

Most of the time we work so hard to find answers
that we can apply to our lives in order to get results.
Jesus is the Answer and we can apply Him to
our lives before we know the results.

Some may say,
"I need answers from Jesus to apply to my situation in order to get results."
The answer is that Jesus is the Answer.
Jesus is the result.
Just apply His name to your situation and you will see results.

Jesus, Your name is the answer even if You don't
tell me any other answers—
even before I see results.
I love You, Lovely One, my Jesus.

87

Transformation

Everything I do is to become a better Kamran.
Now I can see that I don't need to be a better Kamran,
I need to be transformed into the image of Jesus Christ.
I am tired of trying to fix myself using His revelations.
God doesn't need a better Kamran.
He doesn't change me into a better version of myself.
He changes me into Himself.
How can we allow God to change us into His image?

**But we all, with unveiled face beholding as in a mirror the glory of the Lord,
are being transformed into the same image from glory to glory,
just as from the Lord, the Spirit.**

(II CORINTHIANS 3:18)

Sometimes I think to be more like Jesus is to be a better me.
Sometimes we try to help others to be better people
instead of being transformed into the image of Jesus.

We get so satisfied when things get better.
We get satisfied when we see that we are doing
better or becoming better people.
We are satisfied only when we are successful.
When was the last time you checked your
transformation with the Holy Spirit?
We measure ourselves as good or bad, higher or lower.

Holy Spirit, would You show me the level of my transformation?
I am sorry for trying to be a better Kamran for You.
I want to be transformed into Jesus Christ.

88

Growing in God

As Christians we try hard to grow in God but God wants to grow in us.

What does it mean to grow in God?
Does it mean to pursue Him?
Pursue Him for what?
When we find Him, what are we going to do with Him?

I think I got it wrong.
God should grow in me instead of me trying to grow in Him.

Grow in me Jesus, grow in me.

When I look at myself, I don't want to measure my growth in You
but Your growth in me.
My growth has been the center of my attention,
but now I want You and Your growth to become the center.

Help me, God, in Jesus' name.
I am weary and tired from my effort to grow in You.
I have tried to grow up; let me see You growing up in me.
I am called to be a child of God.
I am so sorry for trying to grow up, even in You.
Now I watch You grow in me.
I am excited to watch Your growth in me.

Get as tall and wide as You want to be, God.
How tall do You want to get in me, God?
What are You waiting for?
Set me free from my agony and start Your growth in me.
And please stop what I call "growing in You."

"Enlarge the place of your tent;
Stretch out the curtains of your dwellings, spare not;
Lengthen your cords,
And strengthen your pegs.

"For you will spread abroad to the right and to the left.
And your descendants will possess nations,
And they will resettle the desolate cities"

(ISAIAH 54:2-3)

Let us make room in our hearts for His expansion.

Our Problems Are Here to Fix Us

When we face a difficulty or even our enemies, we have different options.
Most of us run when we face difficulty.
Some will try to go around it.
Some will do nothing with it at all.
They will stand there and look at it, waiting or
hoping it will go away one day.
Few will fight it.
Even fewer will embrace it.

I believe the best way of facing our problems in most cases is to embrace them first.
If we choose to fight our problems before we embrace them,
we are fighting out of our fear.
When we embrace our difficulties, which can be sickness, job loss,
persecution, rejection, misunderstanding, etc.,
the fear will go away and in that stage, if the Lord allow us to fight,
we will fight with so much courage.

The moment we embrace our problems, their power over us will disappear.
Of course, the willingness to embrace a difficulty
should be real and from our hearts,
not just an action of submission with regret.

Once the Lord told me:
"You are not here to fix problems, the problems are here to fix you."

When we embrace our problems, they will do their job,
and when their job is finished they will disappear.
Remember, they are here to fix us, we are not here to fix them.

May the Holy Spirit help us to embrace the
difficulties that He allows to come to us.

In Your beautiful name, Jesus.

90

I Am Who I Am

The Lord told Moses, **"I am who I am" (see Exodus 3:14).**

Who do you say you are, my friend?
How would you introduce yourself?
You will have so much peace when you are comfortable saying,
"I am what I am. I am who I am."
The Lord was comfortable saying, **"I am who I am."**
Are you comfortable saying the same thing?
No matter who you are and what you do, can you say:
"This is it. I can't change myself. *I am who I am*"?

Why should we say that?
We try so hard to change ourselves to be good Christians,
and the more we try, the less results we get.
I can't change myself.
As the Apostle Paul said, "I am the foremost of sinners" (see I Timothy 1:15).

I can say, "I am what I am. I am who I am. I am the foremost of sinners.
Change me, O great I AM."

Worship Starts with Visiting Jesus

During worship we *think* about our love for the Lord.
We use our brains mostly to worship Jesus.
In a very strange way all I see is my face and head during worship.
The focus of my being is my head.
I forget about my body; all I remember is my face.
It seems like I send my brain to visit Jesus,
but Jesus wants all of me, not just my brain.

When you walk, what is the center of your attention?
See, our brains and our eyes are on our faces,
so normally we are fully aware of our faces.
That is why during our worship sometimes all we see is our faces.

When you worship, go with all your body, mind, and spirit to visit Jesus.
To me, worship starts with visiting Jesus in soul, spirit, heart, mind, and body.

Let us practice:
Close your eyes, use your imagination,
and picture your whole body standing in front of Jesus.
Pay attention to your whole body, to your hands, heart, feet, etc.,
standing in front of your beautiful Jesus.

It might sound strange but it will bear good fruits in worship.
Our bodies know their Creator; allow your body to worship its Lord.
We have been limiting our bodies for so long.
Our brains have been the masters of our bodies for so long.
Release your body to worship its Creator.

Help us, Lord.

92

Changed by Love

In the Old Testament, people tried to follow God using the law of God,
and we know that didn't work out very well.
In New Testament living,
most of us as Spirit-filled Christians try to follow God
using the revelations that come from
God and that doesn't work very well either.

In the Old Testament, people tried to
change themselves and others through the law,
and in our time we try to change
ourselves and others through revelations and teachings.
I am in a place where nothing works anymore.
It is not laws or revelations but God's
unconditional love toward me that is changing me.

Laws and revelations will eventually show us
that *nothing can change us but the love of God.*
The unconditional and free love of God is ready to change us all.

Faith Beyond What Christ Reveals

As Christians we all have our own view of Christ.
The question is: Is Christ bigger than our views of Him?
Is He more powerful and beautiful than what we think He is?
If so, then how much bigger, more powerful, and more beautiful?

Most of us walk with Christ in order to get to know Him,
and as He reveals more of His power, might, and beauty to us
then we trust Him and rest in our views of Him.
Our rest depends on the amount of knowledge
and revelation we receive from Him.
Even most of our worship comes out of our personal views of Christ.
We could say the level of our worship is
bound to the level of our knowledge of Christ.
Should we limit Christ to our knowledge of Him?
Should we limit the level of our rest in Christ to what we have seen of Him?
We need to have faith beyond what Christ reveals.

There are things about Christ that will take eternity to know.
There are things about Christ that we will learn forever and ever.
Three things will remain in heaven: hope, faith, and love.
What do we hope for in heaven?
We hope to get to know Christ more.
Why do we need faith in heaven?
There are places in Christ where only faith can fly
to bring us more knowledge and revelation of Him.
Faith will go ahead of us so deep into Christ and even to eternity
and show us so many wonderful things about Christ.

Jesus' disciples were with Him for three years
and Jesus revealed Himself to a degree to them,
but later on He rebuked them for their lack of faith.

Jesus knew that there were places in Him that could be discovered through faith alone and not by Him revealing Himself to His disciples.

What is wrong with Christ revealing Himself to us?
We want to see more of His power, might, glory, and beauty
so we can trust Him more.
There is nothing wrong with Christ revealing Himself to us,
but that place should be the starting point.
Christ is the Beginning and the End.
Our faith can go so fast and so deep into Christ.
Now that He has revealed Himself to a degree to us,
why should we limit Him by what He revealed to us?

We can use our faith and the imagination that He gave us
to see Him as even more beautiful, magnificent, majestic, faithful, giving,
and loving than He has allowed us to see Him so far.

Faith can go to places that no one can go.
Now we can go beyond our own views of God
and even beyond what Christ revealed to us,
using those revelations as a springboard
to embrace faith and jump so much further into Christ.

During our worship we can use what Christ has revealed to us of Himself,
the Father, and the Holy Spirit as a springboard to jump into deeper worship.
I do not know the full level of Christ's beauty,
but with what has been revealed to me,
I can hold onto my faith and imagine a higher level
of the beauty of Christ and worship God.
Now I can imagine a higher level of power and might
through faith and become totally overwhelmed.
Can we go too far imagining God's love and beauty?
No. Never.
No matter how high we jump through
our faith using our imaginations,
we can't touch the end of His love and beauty, because there is no end to His
love, faithfulness, goodness, kindness, might, power, or holiness.

Now I know I am not limited by what
was revealed to me even through Jesus,
but now He is allowing me to add faith and fly so high even to touch **eternity.**
Christ doesn't want us to be limited by what we see.
He doesn't want us to be limited by what we know of Him.
He wants us to ride on faith and allow it to take us to deeper places **in Himself.**

I will be so far behind if I limit Christ with what He reveals to me of **Himself.**
He is giving me faith to go so deep into Him,
and without this new faith there is no way I can get there.

**For this reason I bow my knees before the Father,
from whom every family in heaven and on earth derives its name,**

**that He would grant you, according to the riches of His glory,
to be strengthened with power through His Spirit in the inner man;**

**so that Christ may dwell in your hearts through faith;
and that you, being rooted and grounded in love,**

**may be able to comprehend with all the saints
what is the breadth and length and height and depth,**

**and to know the love of Christ which surpasses knowledge,
that you may be filled up to all the fullness of God.**

(EPHESIANS 3:14-19).

94

Traveling Inside the Truth

Sometimes we find out the truth about something
or someone and we stop there,
but there is no end to the truth and we shouldn't
stop at one point of the truth.
I felt that the Lord showed me *to travel further into the truth*.
We can travel in the truth.
We don't have to stop at one point and come to a conclusion.
Truth is a road that needs to be traveled!
Once you find a truth, don't stop there—keep going further.
Truth will always set you free.
Keep traveling deeper.
Don't settle down with partial truth or a piece of the truth.
Learn to travel deeper.

**"Now in the Law Moses commanded us to stone such women;
what then do You say?"**

**But when they persisted in asking Him, He straightened up, and said to them,
"He who is without sin among you, let him be the first to throw a stone at her."**

(JOHN 8:5-6)

Satan will tell us partial truths about people and stop there.
This brings judgment.
We must keep traveling to get more of the truth.
When the Pharisees brought the adulterous
woman to Jesus and asked His opinion,
Jesus didn't condemn her because He knew
the whole truth and not just the partial truth.
The partial truth was that she got caught in the act of adultery,
but Jesus knew more about both her and the
Pharisees than people were willing to see.
Maybe she never had true love.

Maybe she was abused as a child.
We don't know exactly what Jesus knew about her,
but He knew enough not to judge her.

"For thus says the LORD, 'Your wound is incurable, And your injury is serious.

**'There is no one to plead your cause;
No healing for your sore, No recovery for you.**

**'For I will restore you to health And I will heal you of your wounds,'
declares the LORD..."**

(JEREMIAH 30:12-13, 17)

The Lord told the truth about their wounds not having a cure,
but if we search the Scripture, which reveals more of the truth,
we will see that nothing is incurable for God.
He said there was no healing for their sores,
but He also said that He would heal them.

May we all learn to travel into the truth.
Jesus said, "I am the truth" (see John 14:6).
There is no end to Jesus;
that is one reason He wants us to travel into the truth and never stop.

Lord, we desire to travel into the truth.
We don't want to stop at one point and judge.
Grant us that we may start our travel.
In Your beautiful name, Jesus.

95

Letting Go of the Details

Recently I heard this phrase in my heart:
"the art of letting go of the details for the sake of getting closer to the Master."

Let the Master take care of the details.
Don't let the details drag you here and there, my friend.
A small detail can become a big stumbling block.

Normally this kind of stumbling block will get its way through analyzing
and soon will demand a quick opinion or decision.
Let go of the details as much as possible.
When you start to let go of the details,
you might have to let go of an important one.
But don't worry because the Holy Spirit will guide you
about which details to let go of and which to pay attention to.

For many people, it is their continual sin that keeps them from the Lord,
and for others it is their continual attention to detail.

I don't want to say that paying attention to details is sin,
but paying too much attention to details
can produce the same fruit as sin—
separation from the Father.

Now let's talk about details.
I heard this in my heart:
"Anything but God is a detail."

Now, what do we do with the details?
We lift them up to Jesus.
With the help of the Holy Spirit we will get to the place that anything
but the Father, Son, and Holy Spirit is a detail to us.

96

Flow Between Christ and Us

Jesus made everything about us.
When we make everything about Him,
there will be a flow between Christ and us.
Many of us have been waiting for that flow.
We are supposed to have that flow between Jesus and us.

Jesus said,

"Abide in Me, and I in you"

(SEE JOHN 15:4)

He did His part, now let us do ours and make everything about Christ.
This is a great key to abiding in Him: Make everything about Him.

for if we live, we live for the Lord, or if we die, we die for the Lord;
therefore whether we live or die, we are the Lord's.

(ROMANS 14:8)

Holy Spirit, help us to make everything about Jesus.
Grant us that gift. We want that flow.

97

The Beauty of Pain (Part 1)

Pain is so beautiful, isn't it?

When the Lord reveals someone's deepest pain to us,
it will break our hearts and make our hearts
ready for the love of God to rush in.
What is it about pain that can reflect God's love?
The Lord uses pain, a hated being,
to teach us to love and to get to know His love.
Pain is so hated among us humans.

How does the Lord use pain to teach us about His love?

See, when we hear about God's love,
immediately we try to connect it to ourselves
and wait to see how the Lord will prove His love to us.
Mostly we expect God to show His
love to us through His blessings and favor,
but He will prove His love for us by showing how much He loves
the needy and those whom are so afflicted by pain.
It is not that He loves them more than others,
but He shows His love to us by breaking our hearts for them.
We can pray and ask Him to allow us to feel the pain of the afflicted ones,
and through that we can taste His love.
He uses pain to show His love.

We can hang around those who have so much pain and allow the Lord to break
our hearts for them and show us how much He loves them.
Suddenly they become so beautiful in their pain.
God loves them through us.

There are so many people who have no financial or physical needs
but still have so much pain.

We can start asking our friends about their pain.
We can take this journey of pain—not necessarily
our own pain but the pain of others.
In this journey we will discover God's true
love for others and even for ourselves.

Let us show interest in finding people's pain and gain God's heart for them.
Let us learn how much our Father in heaven loves us all.

O pain, you hated one among us,
we ask that you forgive us for rejecting you.
I am sorry for cursing you.
I cursed the very thing that God sent to show me His love.
Many people hated You, Jesus, the One who came to show God's love,
but You carried all the pain to the very end of Your life.

O pain, allow me to get to know you in me and in the afflicted ones.
You are working in all people.
Allow me to find you in all people.
I am interested in getting to know you.

I have been waiting for so long for God
to show me how much He loves me
through His favor and blessings.
Now I know that by taking this journey of finding out about people's pain,
I can truly understand His love.

*Open the eyes of my heart, Holy Spirit, that I may see the beauty of pain,
and break my heart over it so that I may see Your love.*
Send me to the places with the most pain and affliction
so that I may feel Your love.
I am not ready, but I desire that You make me ready
and give me the honor of breaking my heart.
I am excited to get to know Your love through pain.
Hearts broken over the pain of Your loved ones smells so good to You.
Break our hearts and let the aroma of Your
love through pain come to the surface.

98

The Journey to Understand People's Pain (Part 2)

To me the greatest thing we can do for a person is to see their pain
and to understand how much God loves them.
But in most cases we try to show people how much *we* love them,
and in return we get their approval.
It seems that their knowledge of our love is becoming a need to us.
See, God doesn't get His needs met when one
of us realizes how much He loves us.
He loves us just because He loves us and also wants us to know
that it is for our benefit, not His.
We are the ones who are needy and will do anything to get our needs met.
We even love others and want them to know our love
in order to get our needs met through their approval.
It is a painful struggle to push ourselves to love
others in order to get our needs met.

What do we do then?
I can share my beliefs with you and the rest is between you and Holy Spirit.
I was watching a father who was dancing with
his handicapped son on his arm.
The pain struck my heart and I felt God in that.
I felt God in the pain of another person.
It made me cry and it fed my heart at the same time.
God was feeding my heart through pain
and was showing me His love for that father and son.
It was one of the most beautiful moments of pain that I have ever encountered.
In that moment I didn't have to let those people
know how much I love them;
I had no need of that.
I was getting my need met through the love of God for them
that came to me in the form of another person's pain.
I was speaking that night and I spoke about
the same subject of pain and love.

The father of the handicapped boy came to me after the service with tears in his eyes
and told me that while he was dancing with his son on his arm,
the Lord spoke to his heart about encountering His love
through the pain of the afflicted and broken ones.

We search for the approval of man.
We even search for God's love in blessings and favor,
and He chooses to show His love to us through the pain of another person.
That is why I said earlier that the greatest thing we can do for others
and ourselves is to see people's pain and to understand God's love for them.

*To me, this journey of understanding people's pain and God's love for them
is one of the greatest journeys that mankind can take on earth.*
To a degree this is the same journey that Jesus took.
He came and experienced our pain as a human being
and also showed us how much we are loved by His Father.

Let us ask the Holy Spirit to help us choose
some people and meditate on their lives
to understand their pain and God's love for them.
No more spending our time trying to prove our
love to people to get their approval.
Now we are entering into another season, the season of true love.

People carry so much pain and they are looking for someone
whom they can trust with their pain.
This is the cry of our world.

We are weary from all of our hidden pain.
Is there anyone out there who is interested in our
pain and God's love for us?

Holy Spirit, help us to answer this call.

99

The Proper Medicine at the Proper Time

One day I saw in my heart a picture of a
large warehouse filled with medicine.
The Holy Spirit asked my heart, "What do you see?"
"Medicine," I replied.
He asked, "What is the purpose of medicine?"
"Healing," I replied again.

Then the Holy Spirit opened my eyes to see
something I have never seen before:
Medicine that was made to help heal us can kill us
if we do not pay attention and use wisdom.
We do not need medicine alone—
we also need a doctor who can prescribe the
right medicine according to our needs.

I have a friend who was given the wrong medicine in the hospital and he
almost died. This happens in hospitals and also in our own homes.
Some people take too much medicine on
purpose because they want to die.
The very medicine that was made to heal can be used to kill.

The Bible is filled with medicine and the Holy Spirit is our Doctor.
He will prescribe the proper medicine in the proper time.
We need the Holy Spirit to prescribe what He has already put inside us.
Truth without the guidance of the Holy Spirit can harm people,
like medicine without a doctor's prescription.

Through our walks with God we are filled
with all kinds of revelation and teachings.
We become like big warehouses filled with all kinds of medicine.
But that does not mean we can judge
people's sickness and prescribe it to them.

So many people have been hurt by religious organizations
because of the wrong medicine that was prescribed for them.
Many people don't want anything to do with Christianity
because we have given them the wrong medicine.
If you went to a doctor and he gave you the wrong medicine,
would you want to go back to that doctor?

We should stop writing our own prescriptions and allow the Holy Spirit to
write them. The Lord's medicine must be used in His timing.
He knows the best prescription for every situation.
And of course, never forget that we need
to give out this medicine with love.

We need You, Doctor Holy Spirit.

100

The Crosses of Obedience and Disobedience

There are two kinds of crosses that we face every day:
The cross of obedience and the cross of disobedience.

Every single person is carrying a cross,
even those who don't know God or don't want anything to do with Him.
The cross that comes out of obedience is far easier to carry
and there is so much grace to carry it.
But the cross that comes out of disobedience is hard to bear
and there is no grace to carry it.
Many people are carrying the crosses of their
disobedience every single day.
But Jesus wants us to carry the cross of obedience.
The cross of obedience will lead us into a life of resurrection power.
Carrying the cross of obedience will give us
new, fresh, resurrection life every day.

What is the cross of obedience?
Simply to obey the Lord feels like a cross at first,
like Abraham obeying the Lord's voice to sacrifice Isaac.

Daniel had to face his cross of obedience:

**Then the king gave orders, and Daniel was brought
in and cast into the lions' den.
The king spoke and said to Daniel,
"Your God whom you constantly serve will Himself deliver you."**

(DANIEL 6:16)

Shadrach, Meshach and Abed-nego had to face their crosses:

And he commanded certain valiant warriors who were in his army
to tie up Shadrach, Meshach and Abed-nego,
in order to cast them into the furnace of blazing fire.

What is the cross of disobedience?
It all started from Adam in the garden and there
are many examples in the Bible.
People that don't know God are making many wrong decisions
that will eventually nail them to their crosses.
But even for them there is hope.

When Jesus was on the cross, two thieves were nailed on His right and left side.
Jesus was the only one of the three that was nailed to the cross of obedience,
but when one of the thieves asked Him for help,
Jesus promised him salvation although he was nailed to the cross of
disobedience.
There is always hope even for the ones that are nailed to crosses of
disobedience,
but it is an honor to be nailed to the cross of obedience.
Jesus was nailed to the cross of obedience,
and that led to His resurrection and the salvation of mankind.
May we have the wisdom to recognize the true cross of obedience
and have the courage to carry it.
In His beautiful name.

101

Twisted Truth

When we twist our ankles we experience pain.
Twisted truth will also cause pain.
Satan is causing so many people pain by simply twisting the truth.

There are billions of people on this planet that don't know the truth about
Christ.
So many people want to know God.
So many Muslims are worshiping their god
without knowing the truth about Christ.
*Not knowing the truth or receiving twisted
truth will always cause pain and agony.*
Let us pay more attention to the pain in our lives
and see if the truth was twisted somehow.

Diving Deep into Jesus

When you look into your failures and sin, don't faint.
Learn to look deep into Christ's blood.
The deeper you dive into His blood, the bolder you will become.
Jesus, teach me how to look deep into Your blood.
We can choose to look deep into and meditate on our failures
or to meditate on the blood of Jesus.
One of the thieves that was nailed on the cross beside Jesus
chose to see Him and was saved through His blood.
Even if we are nailed on the cross
like the thief that deserved to be crucified,
let us look upon Jesus and His blood.
The blood that was dripping from the cross saved that thief.
When everything else fails, the blood of Jesus will stand.
When all of our support falls, the blood of Jesus will stand.
When all hell comes after us, the blood of Jesus will stand.
Stay close to the blood.
No matter what kind of season you are in, the blood can protect you.
Cover yourself with the blood.
Dive deep into Jesus.

103

Who Should Ask the Questions?

All my life, Lord, I've asked You questions in order to get answers.
Now would You please ask me questions and give me orders?
I have always asked You questions and told You what I wanted.
Now ask me questions and tell me what You want.

What is He asking us now?
What is He asking the world?

The question the Lord asked Adam and Eve was,

"Where are you?

(SEE GENESIS 3:9)

We always ask Him the same question: "Where are You, God?"

Adam and Eve were in hiding when the Lord asked His question.
Now we think God is in hiding when we ask, "Where are You, God?"
God is not hiding—we are.
He is asking the world, "Where are you?"

The Lord asked Eve,

"What is this you have done?"

(SEE GENESIS 3:13)

Now most of us ask God, "What is it You have done, God?"

Of course, we will always have questions.
But we must stop blaming Him and let Him ask the questions sometimes.
Just listen to His questions.
*I am sure His questions alone will change our
lives even if we do not answer them.*

Walking on Water

Some of us are very good swimmers and are not afraid to swim
even in very deep parts of the ocean.
We think that if we are good swimmers we will
be safe swimming in the ocean,
even when a storm comes.

But there comes a storm that even the best of swimmers
will not last for long in the violence of its waters.
Life can bring storms and no matter how well we swim,
we can be taken by the storm one day.

*We are not called to swim in the storms of our lives,
we are called to walk on them.*
No matter how well trained we become,
we cannot swim and survive in these storms.
Jesus offered us something much higher than swimming.
He wants to teach us to walk on water.

How do we walk on water through the storms of our lives?
By simply looking into His face and having faith in Him.
Peter did it for a short time.
No matter how much you improve your ability to swim,
you will be caught in the storm one day and your
swimming skills will be no help at all.
We need to learn to walk on water.

Let's spend our time looking at His face
instead of spending our time on more swimming lessons.
Let's have simple faith in Him without analyzing our situations.
The more we analyze and think,
the less chance we have to walk on the water.
Aren't you tired of analyzing?

Aren't you tired of swimming and teaching others to swim?
Aren't you tired of judging people for their lack of swimming skills?
There is one possible way to walk on water,
and all other efforts are just a waste of time and energy.

Let us zoom in on His face and walk on
the water that we face every single day.
We will be tempted to use our swimming skills in the oceans of our lives.
We must get ready to walk on water before the storm hits.
Jesus is calling us to walk on the water.
Refuse to use your swimming skills.
Help us, Holy Spirit, to stop swimming and start
walking on water even in the storm.
I count on You, Holy Spirit.

105

Your Uniqueness and Grace (Part 1)

Once the Lord showed this to my heart:
Obedience is following the path of grace.
Grace always calls for uniqueness.

The Lord made each of our minds and hearts very unique.
To follow grace requires us to stay who we are
in our own uniqueness of mind and heart.

We don't need to shape and alter our uniqueness
to fit into our surroundings.
We don't have to be like others, even when their uniqueness
is so attractive and fruitful.

Allow grace to be the mentor of your uniqueness
and shape your raw uniqueness
into a mature and beautiful one.
What you call the grace and favor of the Lord on some people's lives
is simply the fruit of their mature uniqueness.
May the Lord bear so much fruit out of our uniqueness of mind and heart.

My friend, enjoy the grace of our Lord Jesus Christ.
Enjoy the fellowship of God's grace through your own individual uniqueness.
God designed a special grace to fit your own uniqueness.
God loves you enough to give you your own designer clothing.
Follow grace. Enjoy her fellowship.
Help us, Holy Spirit.

Once I heard in my heart,
"Follow Lady Grace."

I knew that the Lord was talking about the Holy Spirit.
The Holy Spirit can be always found in our lives through our uniqueness.

Give permission to your uniqueness to come out and grow
despite people's rejection and unbelief.
Meet Lady Grace in your own uniqueness.

106

True Christianity and Uniqueness (Part 2)

True Christianity can be found in our uniqueness.
Christianity should not be a religion where we all follow our God
in the same way and manner.
Christ is so alive and our Christianity should be as well.
That is the beauty of true Christianity.

Now let's talk about true Christianity.
What is true Christianity?
Let me say first what I believe is not true Christianity.
If we don't stay true to ourselves and our own uniqueness,
that is not true Christianity.
When we give our hearts to Christ,
He doesn't come to take away our personalities and uniqueness
but to work on them and show Himself through them.
We don't have to give up our personalities and uniqueness.
We just need to be willing for the Holy Spirit to alter them.
Be yourself my friend, be yourself as much as you desire.
The Holy Spirit will rush out of you when you
stay true to yourself and your uniqueness.

Don't allow people, religion, fear, or needs to change your personality
and uniqueness and make you into something you are not.

Do you want to share Christ with others?
Do you want Christ to come out of you and meet people?
Then stay true to yourself and build up your uniqueness
with the help of the Holy Spirit.
The Holy Spirit is very unique.
We were created in God's image and God wants us to be unique like Him.

And God created man in His own image, in the image of God He created him;
male and female He created them.

(GENESIS 1:27)

Christ came, not to give us something new,
but to restore what was stolen from us in the fall.

**For those whom He foreknew,
He also predestined to become conformed to the image of His Son,
that He would be the first-born among many brethren**

(ROMANS 8:29).

See, Father God is very unique.
So are Jesus and the Holy Spirit.
THE GODHEAD IS VERY UNIQUE.

How can I enjoy God if I don't stay as unique as He made me to be?
He is restoring us to this place of uniqueness in His image.

Systems will always to try to make us all the same.
Systems will try to take away our unique personalities.
There is no joy in religious systems.
If I don't enjoy my Christianity then I will be trapped by religion.
If we don't enjoy our own personalities and uniqueness,
we cannot enjoy God at all.
Religion will try to change our personalities and uniqueness
so much that we cannot enjoy ourselves at all.

Don't be embarrassed by your uniqueness and personality;
if you are then you will be embarrassed by God in you.
One of the reasons that we are embarrassed to share Christ with others
is that deep down inside we are embarrassed
of our own personalities and uniqueness.
When you enjoy who you are then you will enjoy sharing who you are with
others,
and through that you will share Christ with others.
The more you enjoy your personality and uniqueness,
the more you can share Christ with others.
Let us enjoy ourselves and in that enjoy
God and share Him with others with joy.

107

Perverted Judgments

Is it possible that a judgment can be more perverted than a perverted act?
I believe it can.

Let us be more careful in our judgments toward others.
Let us not be so quick to judge.
We are all capable of falling into perverted judgment.

Jesus didn't judge the adulterous woman, but the Pharisees did.
I believe their judgment was more perverted
than the act of her adultery itself.
They were using their own judgment against
her to prove that Jesus was wrong.

How many times do we judge others to make ourselves feel good
and prove our own self-righteousness?
When the Lord judges us it is for our own good.
He does it because He loves us so much.
All He does, even His anger, judgment, and rebuke
is based on His unconditional love for us.
If we judge one another to prove our own self-righteousness,
that judgment will be perverted.
It is not okay to encourage sin, but neither is it okay to use perverted
judgment.

We are all guilty and we all need Jesus.
May the Lord forgive us all.
He is so forgiving and so beautiful.
We love You, Jesus.

108

Cleansing Our Hearts

It is a sad thing to hear of someone getting
sentenced to prison, tortured, or killed.
Have you ever sentenced anyone to be in prison,
or to be tortured and killed?
Many of us would say no.

I believe many of us have done these very things.
How have we done them?
In our hearts.
We are all capable of having prisons, torture
chambers, and graveyards in our hearts.

Prison

A prison is "a building (or vessel) to which people are legally committed
as a punishment for crimes they have committed or while awaiting trial"
(Apple Dictionary).

Does that sound familiar?
Have you ever imprisoned people who wronged you in your heart?
It is so easy to judge others and sentence them to prison in our hearts.
When we hold judgment against others,
we make them prisoners of our hearts.
I have done this personally.

Torture

An act of torture can be infliction of pain, abuse, ill treatment,
persecution, or any other sadistic act.

Torture is defined as "the action or practice of
inflicting severe pain on someone

as a punishment or to force them to do or say something,
or for the pleasure of the person inflicting the pain;
great physical or mental suffering or anxiety;
a cause of such suffering or anxiety"
(Apple Dictionary).

When I judge my wife in my heart,
she can feel and see it in my eyes even if I don't say it out loud.
I can see how my judgment tortures her.
People are sensitive enough to feel the judgment in our hearts against them.

Grave

A grave is "a place of burial for a dead body,
typically a hole dug in the ground and marked by a stone or mound"
(Apple Dictionary).

We are capable of sentencing to death the people who wronged us
and creating graveyards in our hearts where we bury them.
How many times have we said:
"That person is dead to me.
I don't want to have anything to do with that person anymore"?

Do we want our hearts to become prisons, torture chambers, or graveyards?
Absolutely not.

It terrifies me to know that I have some dead bodies
in the graveyard of my heart.
It also terrifies me to know that I even have a graveyard,
prison, or torture chamber in my heart.

The enemy with all his accusation toward other people wants to make prisons,
torture chambers, and graveyards out of our hearts.
The Lord with His love and forgiveness toward us and others
wants to make a beautiful garden of His love in our hearts.

You are a gardener, Jesus.
We give You our hearts every single day to work in them.
We want our hearts to be a place that people can come in and have fun,
get free, and experience You and Your love and forgiveness.
Cleanse our hearts, Lord.

109

Get Your Heart Involved

God is calling us out of our depression, hopelessness, and fear.
How?
By getting our hearts involved.

Is it possible to talk, breathe, think, see, smell, and hear through our hearts?
Yes, I believe it is.
How?

Talk

Talk to others in your quiet time while they are not there with you.
Start talking to them as if they were standing in front of you.
Try to use your heart instead of your mind.
Instead of picturing them in your mind, try to picture them in your heart.
Get your heart involved as much as possible.
Try this method every day.
Pick someone whom you are having a hard time with.
Picture them in your heart, and talk to them through your heart.
Let your heart call out their names.
Let your heart communicate to its Creator.

Breathe

Try to breathe through your heart.
It is not as hard as you think.
It is very relaxing.
Just picture your heart and take a deep breath
and pay attention to your heart.
There is not a logical explanation of how to do this, but if you try,
the Holy Spirit will guide you and get your heart involved.

Think

It is very powerful when we think of others in our hearts.
It is very powerful to think through our hearts about everything.
Just use your imagination and see others in your heart.
When we fall in love with someone, we cannot help
but to think of them in our hearts.
We can use the same principle and see those
whom we don't necessarily love through our hearts.

Smell

When we try to smell through our hearts, even using our noses,
we go to a higher level of enjoyment.
Try to give all your attention to the smell of a flower.

Hear

Try to hear a song through your heart.
Try to hear people and listen to what they say through your heart.

Normally our brains will subconsciously do all of the above actions.
We have trained them to do so.
Now we can get our hearts involved in our five senses.

It is so incredible and freeing to be able to use our hearts
and get them involved in all these things.

Some of us haven't been using our hearts for so long.
Some of us have been so hurt that it caused us
to close the doors of our hearts
with chains and heavy-duty locks.

Jesus is calling us to open our hearts to Him
and get our hearts involved with each other *and* our enemies.
Some of us have been asking God for an open heaven.
An open heart is an open heaven because Christ lives in us as Christians.
When we open our hearts, heaven will be open also.

Some may feel it is very painful to open their hearts.
Yes, it is hard to show our hearts to others and use them in everyday life,
but it is much harder to put our hearts in prison
and build walls around them for protection.

Allow your heart to come out more often.
Allow your heart to breathe.
Release your heart and let it grow and experience life.

Our hearts need to love and to be loved.
If you feel you have no one who loves you,
start loving someone in your heart and your heart will be so satisfied.
As I mentioned before,
you can start by imagining some people in your heart who hurt you.
Start talking to them in your heart.
You can even tell them about your disappointment.
Remember to get your heart involved.
After a while, you will start to see them and what they did to you
with the eyes of your heart and most of
your judgment and pain will go away.

When we get our hearts involved, the healing possibilities are endless.
True joy will come to us through our hearts.

We gave our hearts to the Son of God through the Spirit;
let us now give our hearts to the sons of man—each other.

Our hearts need to be connected to the heart of the Son of God
and also to the hearts of the sons of man.

110

Heart Work

Work hard and set your mind and heart on your work.
But remember, your life is not just your work.

Meditate on your spouse, family members, and neighbors in your heart.
If you stop meditating and don't remember them in your heart,
then work will take over your heart.
There are many good things to meditate on.

Meditate in your heart every day on:
God's grace, God's love, God's mercy, God's holy fear, God's power,
the cross and what happened there, communion, and other uplifting things.

We always are encouraged to work hard
by looking at the lives of people who have accomplished so much.
Our hard work is always encouraged, but let's do some heart work.

111

Tell Me Something Romantic

How is Your heart, God?
Do You have any pain in Your heart?
Do You have any eager desires in Your heart?
Is there anything Your children can do to minister to Your heart?

You will fulfill the desires of Your children's hearts.
Who is going to fulfill the desires of Your heart?

"Tell me something romantic," He said.

His heart desires romance.
He gave us romance.
He is the master of romance.
He is in love.
Our God is in love.

Romance is what You want, but Is this a time of romance?
When the world is upside down, how can You think of romance?
Romance is for times of happiness.
Now there is so much pain everywhere.

Tell me again Lord, what do You desire?
"Your heart," He said.

But Lord, can I give You something else instead?
Tell me again, what do You desire, Lord?
How do You feel about the current world situation?
How do You feel about Your body, the church?
How do You feel about Muslims worshiping Allah?
How do You feel about Buddhists and their beliefs?

How is Your heart doing, Lord?
What are Your desires?

"Tell me something romantic," He said.

Why romance?
What can I do for You, Lord?
Tell me something to do.

"Constantly I ask you for your heart and constantly you offer me your hand,"
He said.
"I want your heart."

What are You going to do with my heart, Lord.

I will change the nations with your heart."

Tell me something to do, I repeated.

"*Tell me something romantic.*" He said.

End Note:

Thank you for being with us in this journey of the heart.

If your heart was touched by this book, we ask that you might consider helping us to get this message out into the world around you.

How can you help?

By telling family members, friends and coworkers about this book.

By purchasing extra copies of this book and giving them away.

By asking your local church, colleges and organizations to have this book available at their bookstores.

For information about purchasing this book or
for speaking engagements with Kamran go to

www.Projectcallout.org